ME AND MY ANGEL

by
Bob Eastman

*"Reading time is not too long . . .
but it took almost my whole life to take place."*

ROBERT D. REED PUBLISHERS • BANDON, OR

Robert D. Reed Publishers
P. O. Box 1992
Bandon, OR 97411
Phone: 541/347-9882 • Fax: -9883
E-mail: 4bobreed@msn.com
www.rdrpublishers.com

Book design: Marilyn Yasmine Nadel
Cover design: Michelle Sinclair & Grant Prescott
Editor: Angela Berbaum

ISBN: 1-931741-45-x
Library of Congress Card Number: 2004092758

Produced and Printed in the United States of America

Dedication

This book is gratefully dedicated, with love, to my friends and family members that urged me to put down on paper, the many things I had told them about my 'Angel' and our long and close relationship.

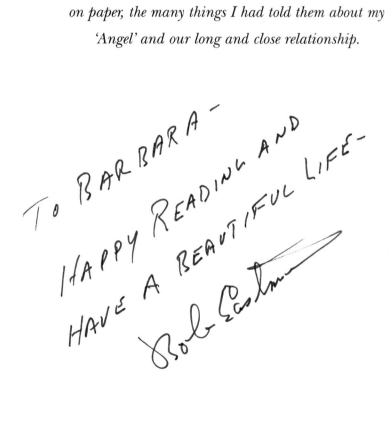

TO BARBARA —
HAPPY READING AND
HAVE A BEAUTIFUL LIFE —
Bob Eastman

ALLIANCE
CHICAGO
GANDER
BANGOR
BLYTHEVILLE MACON
NASHVILLE
SAN PEDRO
AUSTIN
MONTGOMERY
ARCADIA

BROKEN LINE — AIR ROUTE

SOLID LINE — WATER OR RAIL ROUTE

OUR BEAUTIFUL "EARTH", THAT
I WAS FORTUNATE ENOUGH TO BE ABLE
TO SEE, EXPERIENCE AND CIRCLE,
WHILE SERVING OUR BEAUTIFUL
COUNTRY, THE "UNITED STATES OF AMERICA."
"THANKS TO ALL".
Bob Eastman

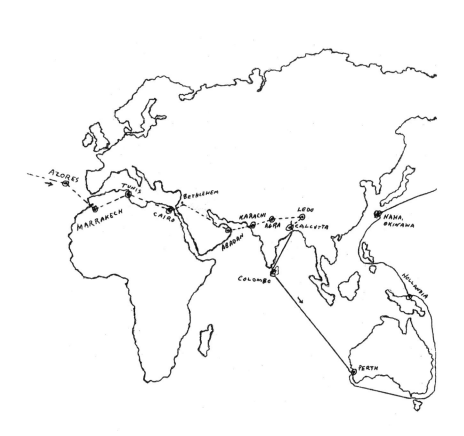

AZORES

TUNIS

BETHLEHEM

MARRAKECH   CAIRO

KARACHI   LEDO

AGRA   CALCUTTA

ABADAN

COLOMBO

NAHA,
OKINAWA

HOLLANDIA

PERTH

Brand new pilot.
Just flew my first solo flight.

Chapter One

Once upon a time, a long time ago, there was a young boy that was about to begin an adventure — an adventure that was to be "the adventure of his life." In fact, the adventure was the beginning of the rest of his life. He walked into the neighborhood United States Army Recruiting Office, and the first of many pages of this adventure story came into being.

The time was in the year 1942; the place was Chicago, Illinois. The era was that of World War II. The young boy was me, a bright, shiny, 20-year old. The time now is in the year 2002. The young boy is still me, still bright, though not quite as shiny. However, the lack of luster is more than made up by the weight of wisdom (I think!).

As a little kid, I chose airplanes and flying as my dream material instead of fire engines, choo-choo trains or police squad cars. Model airplanes grew into the real thing when I signed up as an Aviation Cadet, reported for duty, learned to fly a Stearman Primary Trainer Bi-Plane, took the real plunge of soloing, and then went on to basic training where the airplanes looked like real "war planes" (minus guns).

Those of us that lived the days of Hitler speeches, London bombings, submarine sinkings, Pearl Harbor, war-time movies and news reels, remember the breathless thinking and planning and waiting and finally the doing of the things of destiny. In my case, the boy model airplane builder all of a sudden becoming a man in the cockpit of a real airplane seems like reading fictional writing, but it was true.

Flight training was a time of true excitement with all the new sound, feel, sight, smell and thought. The thrill of just being there was almost too much to be able to believe. And as I put these thoughts down on paper, bring back goose bumps of memory onto my flesh.

I am so lucky to have these memories. But wait, these memories have more to them than pure nostalgia. When you dig into them and examine each one time after time, they are like a string of pearls. Each memory is a pearl with a value of its own.

My first memory of my new flight experience took place in a wonderful part of our country, Arcadia, Florida. Not really having been any place in my young life, except the Chicago area, Florida was the most romantic place on Earth.

I'll never forget the unexpected, magical aroma of orange blossoms, wafting through the open railway windows of the troop train, taking me to my new life. Indescribable weariness, brought on by slow travel between Nashville, Tennessee and Arcadia, Florida, in a sitting position for about twenty hours, miraculously disappeared with the building excitement of getting close to my primary flight training air base in Arcadia. Even the name "Arcadia" was different from anything I had ever heard.

It was still dark outside the troop train, but I knew it couldn't be much farther if the air smelled so sweet. It actually took quite a lot more time, but I didn't mind.

Primary flight training proved to be all that I had dreamed of for such a long time. The Stearman P-17 Primary trainer turned out to be a perfect introduction to the "world of the birds." An open cockpit with wings that could take you through any kind of maneuver did indeed make you feel akin to your feathered friends. Then add two months of example flying with a master pilot, and you felt you could do anything a bird could do, and then some. About the only thing that was left out was the laying of an egg.

I reached the thrill of solo flight in no time, and soon was ready for basic training. Basic is what I wanted with heavier airplanes, so that I could begin to train for what I had enlisted for, but I always missed the pure joy and freedom I had found in flying the Stearman.

*My primary flight training class. My instructor,
T. Myrle Kitchens, is in the center.*

Stearman PT-17 Primary Flight Trainer.

Chapter Two

Looking back through the dim past, an early memory seems to stand out, as if floodlights were helping to separate and make clear the picture being told. I was flying a blue and yellow low wing basic trainer called the BT-13, which we nicknamed "The Vultee Vibrator" because of its noisy characteristics. My flying time this morning was devoted to causing my plane to fall into an intentional tailspin and then to recover from the spin. The saying goes, "Practice makes perfect," and the practice spin recoveries were going well, until all of a sudden I found that my big "air machine" would not answer to my bidding. The tailspin continued no matter how many times I tried to recover to a normal dive, and the altimeter kept on informing me that the ground was getting closer and closer, not that I needed to be told that fact. The picture was in front of me with all the horror you can imagine. One last failed try at recovering, and then I reached for the canopy release handle intending to bail out. I had always said that I did not want to parachute. Why practice something that had to be perfect the first time? I had been glad that we weren't required

Vultee B-13 Basic Flight Trainer.

to jump as part of our training and thought that I'd wait until the time I had to bail out. Well, this was that time — except the damned canopy would not slide open! I pulled and tugged with all my might, but it wouldn't budge. Something was wrong and that was the story!

I went back to trying to get out of the tailspin — and what do you know — the plane just kind of staggered out of the spin all by itself, and I just kind of weakly leveled out my flight and flew around in complete disbelief of all the happenings. I tried to slide the canopy open and of course, NOW it opened without a hitch. The fresh, cold air rushing onto my perspiration felt so good!

How did my tailspin stop spinning? A good question, I guess. There are probably numerous answers, however, without much worry about it, I just simply said, "Thank you, God" and let it go at that. Then as life went on and one question after another came up, the plot grew deeper and very interesting. Please note the title of these writings, and you will see where I'm headed.

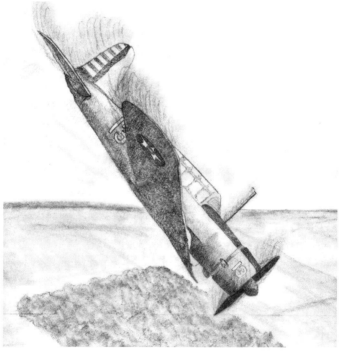

The tailspin I don't want to try again

Chapter Three

Many hours of flight and study, and fun too, came and went with graduation the end result. The silver wings and lieutenant bars were worth all the effort, making the proud day a great one. I felt that too many of my friend cadets "washed out" and didn't make the ultimate goal of pilot's rating, but having made it through thick and thin seemed all the sweeter because of the difficult victory.

We all felt that we were hot shot pilots by now, but of course we were more like the baby birds just kicked out of the nest by our wise mom. And it didn't take long for our instructors to show us the way. Also, it didn't take long for us to appreciate all of their efforts, as the reality of our war training sank in.

The Mitchell B-25. The aircraft that my orders said I would be flying at Maxwell Field, Montgomery, Alabama. I was elated and couldn't wait to start flying with this "hot" beauty.

The Liberator B-24.
This is the aircraft that I found out I would be flying at Maxwell Field. It was a heavy bomber. There had been a "slight" typographical error.

The Douglas C-47.

The Douglas C-47.
This is the aircraft that I was finally assigned to fly. I hadn't done well with the B-24, so my instructor, being a real good guy, saw to it that I was transferred to Bergstrom Field, Austin, Texas. I was very happy; a good airplane.

My crew alongside a C-47 at Blytheville, Arkansas Replacement Training Center.
Left to right: Sgt. Guerra (Radio Operator), Lt. Cassella (Co-Pilot),
Sgt. Brown (Crew Chief), and me.

Replacement training was where we found out what our flying was all about. Our crews were put together: First Pilot, Co-Pilot, Crew Chief, Navigator, Radio Operator; and we flew together all the time to learn and perfect all of our skills that would be needed in order to save our necks when we would soon be in the big picture. It's hard to know what we felt then. Were we scared underneath our outer manner, or were we numb to all the "goings-on?" I honestly can't answer that question. To me now, it all seems like another world that I saw and remember like a movie, but didn't actually take part in.

One nice bright and sunny day a flight of us (three aircraft, C-47 transports, twin-engine planes built by Douglas and in the command of U.S. Army Troop Carrier) were learning the ins and outs of formation flying in our new birds. We had all flown in formation before, but never like this.

When a pilot flies formation with another aircraft, he should try to fly close in to that aircraft, remain steady no matter what, and duplicate the other's maneuvering like you were glued together. In order to accomplish this feat, you must concentrate and never take your eyes off the aircraft that you are in formation with.

So you can see that the size and type of airplane can make a lot of difference in how you fly formation. It's about like the difference between a Porsche sports car and a Greyhound bus. Then add some turbulence along with poor visibility and you have the picture of why we had to learn how and then practice, practice, practice.

Single engine is a lot different from big multiengine with all the weight and people on board. I know personally of the responsibility I all of a sudden felt, knowing that I was lucky enough to be designated as a First Pilot and had to fly formation with two other big planes, acting like I knew what I was doing and doing a good job. I feel like sweating just thinking about it.

But wait! That's not the whole story! After sweating around the skies of Alliance, Nebraska for I don't know how long, we successfully completed our training flight, headed back for the field at our airbase, and individually entered the landing pattern. My Crew Chief, Co-Pilot and I all saw it at about the same time… "it" being black smoke trailing from our starboard engine. What an ugly sight! My call to the tower brought calm directions to continue my landing procedure. Believe me, I needed to hear a calm voice at a time like that.

My landing and taxiing to the parking tarmac were routine, even though my heartbeat and breathing weren't. As soon as the engines were shut down, red flames shot up from the engine nacelle and cast their color on us in the cockpit. Then there was the "SWOOSH" sound as the flames were doused and killed by the on-board fire extinguisher foam that my Crew Chief thoughtfully set off. Brownie saved me a lot of criticism by the timely pulling of the fire extinguisher control. I should have done that as it was my duty, but he backed me up and earned my gratitude.

No great damage done, important lessons learned, experience chalked up; and upon examination of what had happened, a pattern seemed to be forming that would be more evident as time went by. This time my loyal and dependable Crew Chief got into the act along with the apparent "Angel" on board with us.

Chapter Four

The powers that be must have looked at their schedules, and realizing that we were ready and were needed at the big show, passed on the orders to all of us to pack up and go to Bear Field at Fort Wayne, Indiana. This was real excitement! We were about to be issued brand new airplanes! Can you imagine a bunch of kids getting new airplanes to fly to an adventure in another part of the world! This kind of experience is actually beyond expressing with mere words. You had to be there.

Days and weeks of familiarization with our new bird and new equipment sped by, with our personal lives injected whenever possible.

All the new aircraft given to aircrews like us had long identification numbers on the vertical stabilizer. Our I.D. ended in 623, so that was part of our radio call sign. My personal I.D. name was "Giggle Victor." Can you imagine flying halfway around the world as "Giggle Victor?"

We were so fortunate to be where we were in that time and place. I used the opportunity to convince the love of my life that she should marry me! She did! Happy Days!

Guess what? A wonderful chaplain at the airbase somehow heard of our wedding and arranged to have an order change for my whole crew, giving us an extra month in Fort Wayne. How about that for a wedding present? The rest of my crew didn't mind the extra time stateside either. I don't remember what they did, but I'm sure they didn't waste the bonanza.

After too short a honeymoon, I waved good-bye (or I should say "hasta la vista") and got into my new airplane and flew away. We made it to Bangor, Maine for our last footsteps on the good old U.S.A. Next stop for three days was Gander Field, Newfoundland, which was to be our jumping off place for the trans-Atlantic flight. That last night's sleep was a nervous one and also short as take-off was scheduled for something like 0400. Still at Gander, but in a black, cold, windy, snow-covered morning, we were all trying to ready our plane for take-off. Ole' 623 didn't want to wake up no matter how hard my Crew Chief, Brownie, and I coaxed her. At least I was up in the cockpit out of the wind, but poor Brownie was out in the frigid world doing everything that he knew how to do, and he finally did it. The starboard engine coughed and putted, and then roared out loud. Then soon the port engine followed suit and the resulting duet was beautiful music to hear.

Our landing out somewhere in all that water was to be made in the Azores, a little dot of islands that we hoped to find, and we did of course. But if you can imagine the situation we were in, we didn't know where we were going. Our orders for beyond the Azores were sealed, and we were not to open them until a certain distance was reached. We had assumed that we were headed for Europe, so England was our logical destination (you should never assume anything). Being habitually disciplined, I insisted on waiting to open the orders. Finally the glorious sun was up and sparkling the vast ocean beneath us. One of us (I don't remember who) tore open the big manila envelope and guess what? We were ordered to the C.B.I. (standing for the China-Burma-India theatre) and not Europe. I'm sure we must have been breathless at the news that we were beginning a trip half way around the world. The adventure of all of this was hard to believe, but as it turned out for us, the big important thing about our piece of news was that we missed all of the flying during the Normandy invasion. The crews that we would have left with a month earlier all participated in airdrops of paratroopers over France during the night hours before the big invasion hit the beaches. Later when we found out about all the guys that didn't make it that night, it was a sobering realization of just how lucky we were. I know that I felt that way. We didn't talk about it much. A welcome letter from my best pilot friend, who was also a First Pilot and flew during that horrible night, told me he made it O.K. Also I'm glad to be able to say that he made it through the whole war. I lost track of him and couldn't correspond, but found out about his safe return from someone else.

Just think what a fantastic wedding present my whole crew and my bride and I received from that wonderful anonymous chaplain. You can't tell me that my Angel wasn't doing a good job that day!

Chapter Five

Surprise! We found the Azores. Good work by our young navigator and radio instruments made routine out of the task. Another surprise was the foreign language used by the ground crew as they went about securing our aircraft. It turned out to be Portuguese, a sure sign that we were a long way from our "home sweet home."

I don't remember much about the remainder of our first day on the Azores, except the softly warm ocean breeze, while standing alongside a weather beaten tree on the edge of a cliff overlooking a sandy beach being lapped by gentle waves. The rest is all lost in a welcome night's sleep. I know that I was sooooooo tired!

After a day or so of rest and briefing, we made an early morning takeoff. I'm glad to be able to say that it wasn't so early that it was still dark. The sun was up, everything looked quite beautiful, with the exception of a rather large and heavy toolbox sitting right in the middle of our runway. Seeing it and avoiding it was luckily accomplished. If not, it would have either delayed or cut short our just-beginning adventure. Why would a big toolbox be in a place like that? We were the first plane off that morn-

ing, why didn't someone check that runway at dawn? I can remember doing just that myself on other days, racing up and down the runways at first light in an open jeep, as the regular duty of the "Air Drome Officer."

Anyway, the incident turned out to be harmless and the tower operator thanked me for the information I gave, and I'm sure that the obstacle was removed pronto. Another disaster avoided and added to a growing list.

I do believe that I owe a grateful "thank you" to my Angel as I now look back on all these close ones in my wonderful lifetime. Hindsight is 20/20 as they say, and this look back is certainly clear.

Chapter Six

Our next stop was at a romantic sounding place in our world, Marrakesh, Morocco. The only spot that would have sounded more romantic would have been Casablanca, due to the great movie of the same name and time period. I can hear the music and lyrics of "As Time Goes By" through my mind's ear as I write these words. Reminiscences are such a fantastic part of one's life. How hollow it would be without them, and how blessed we are with their riches.

The coast of West Africa rose out of the blue Atlantic with Marrakesh surrounded by a seemingly endless sea of sand. A dazzling sight in the blazing sunlight and seeing Africa lying ahead of us brought home the reality of what we were doing.

Probably the balance of two days was the length of our stay in Morocco; I think it was enough, considering. Not being a real tourist at heart, I guess I missed a lot of sights, as there were numerous opportunities during the free time of the days and evenings. On this arrival day, I chose to stick close to the base and our plane, while the rest split in different directions. After dinner, as nighttime fell, I decided to sleep in the plane, providing an all-night watch. Something about the place gave me an uneasy feeling. As it turned out, all was quiet and I had a good night's sleep, but when the next evening came, I joined a group for dinner and local nightlife of a kind. Crew Chief Brownie drew watch on the line with our plane.

Bright and early the next morning, we headed across North Africa with the destination being Tunis. Another one of those names that draws pictures of a ringed oasis with palm trees and fresh water in an otherwise parched desert with no life to be seen except camels and French Foreign Legionnaires.

Instead of the above, what we saw ahead of us was the build-up of a lot of inclement weather. Our weather briefing had acquainted us with the possibility of some rough air enroute, so it was no surprise. What was a surprise I found when I went back into the cargo bay to get something out of my B-4 bag (a bag that each of us had, packed with all our personal belongings, clothes, toiletries, etc.) and found NO BAG! That is correct. There was no B-4 bag at all where I had placed it near the exit door so many days ago. I know that it had been sitting there the day before when I had taken something out and put something in. But there was no B-4 bag there now. I looked all over, thinking it had been moved, but no such luck. I did find everyone else's B-4 bag, but not mine.

The ensuing conversation between all of us turned up the woeful fact that Brownie had left the plane briefly during the night, for I forget what, and during that time some "so and so" character reached into the cabin and took the closest thing he found, MY B-4 bag. You can bet that I called him stronger things than "so and so"; unfortunately that didn't get my bag back.

I could have raised hell with Brownie. He was supposed to guard the airplane, but he felt so bad about the theft, I couldn't see any point in it. He was my friend and after all, we relied upon each other all the time for the safety of our very lives. So I radioed back to Marrakesh, hoping that the bag would be sent to me if it ever was found. It never was.

When the dust cleared, the thought came to me later that my not making a big thing over Brownie's mistake was a good balancing deed for Brownie's quick covering up of my not pulling the fire extinguisher control during our engine fire, way back when. I told him so and thanked him again.

Needless to say, I soon got tired of wearing the same soiled flight clothes during the rest of our trip. Washing socks and underwear nightly became routine.

The "so-and-so: taking my bag.

Chapter Seven

The balance of our flight from Marrakesh to Tunis was far from routine. The predicted rough weather was indeed rough, and we found ourselves penetrating frontal conditions with no chance of climbing over or going around any of the high build-ups of thunderheads. Since we were climbing over the Atlas Mountains, we couldn't even think of trying to fly low enough to remain contact. As they say, "Never fly through a stuffed cloud," meaning don't fly into a mountain! So we toughed it out on instruments and navigation.

It's good to be able to say the whole crew would have made good sailors. Not one even felt slightly seasick, or any kind of sick, and it wasn't that the elements didn't try to rough us up. The only casualty was me with a bump on the head. While making my way from the cockpit to the navigator's station, we hit a violent down draft that raised my feet right off the flight deck and brought my head into immediate contact with the upper surface of the fuselage. I'm glad that section had no sharp projections reaching out to draw my blood. Just a little bump I could handle.

One plane of our group that was proceeding to Tunis that day was actually flipped over on its back, going through that exact same weather front! Thanks to GOD, they and all the rest of us made it in one piece that day. I was especially grateful when we finally reached the Algiers Air Space. The "socked in" cloud condition suddenly changed, and as the clouds parted, I could see the airfield below. What a beautiful sight that was! I had been sweating out my preparations for an instrument letdown for some time as we approached the point where it would be necessary. I had made many such instrument landing approaches in training conditions.

First we used "link trainers" (a mock up model of an aircraft that looked and acted like the real thing when you were sitting in the cockpit during training). When you had learned the system of flying patterns and reacting to radio signals, you managed to "land" the make-believe air-

The parted clouds reveal the airstrip just in time.

plane on the imaginary runway without ever looking at anything but your pretend charts and instruments.

When you went through the simulation enough, so that your instructor thought you might know enough to try the real thing, he said, "O.K. Let's go out and try the real thing." Of course you didn't wait for a rainy day, but you did fly your real plane, with the instructor in the co-pilot's seat. Everything was real except the weather, and it was "no fair" to look out the window to see where you were. You had to fly only by looking at your instrument panel and recognizing radio signals.

When you were on your final approach and had reached a pre-designated altitude in your let down, you pretended that you had broken through the cloud cover and could see the runway, and then you could look out the windshield and land the big bird.

Doing the real instrument landing approach would have been a too-exciting finale to our already exciting day. I just loved seeing that welcome runway on the concrete. What a day! Could my Angel have had anything to do with the last minute parting of the clouds over that North African airfield?

After securing our aircraft, good ole' 623, and reporting and debriefing at operations, relaxation and food were in order. Also, some planning could be heard for early evening nightlife, which would probably be limited to the USO, non-com clubs, and officer's clubs. The next day there could be some sightseeing and maybe even a tour of the Casbah, a notoriously infamous Old Tunis section of bars, shops, etc., which I'm sure was mostly off limits for our guys. As for me, I was bushed to say the least, and some shut-eye was right on the top of the list. Especially after the burglary experience in Morocco, I decided that I would simplify the standing watch system and just take it all myself. It would be a lying down, sleeping with one eye open watch, but our stuff would be secure and our guys could enjoy and relax. As it turned out, during the rest of our trip air base security was excellent, and we could all relax in assigned quarters.

Chapter Eight

Two days in Tunis gave all of us a nice rest, and our faithful "bird" had a good mechanical going-over, so as we hit the skies again, all was well. The world kept passing beneath us as we kept winging to the East; always heading toward new sights and new challenges.

The intensely blue sky of Tunisia began to change as we approached the vast expanse of the Sahara Desert. Our weather briefing had covered the possibility of blowing sand, and we could see the sandy color taking over the sky above us until it looked much like what was beneath us. Soon the thickness of the air around us rivaled fog, and we were flying on instruments again. Climbing to higher altitude didn't offer relief, so we tried it down lower. The terrain being relatively flat, we slowly let down and were rewarded with welcome contact conditions.

One real concern flying through all that sand was, "How good are the filters on our engines?" I guess they were pretty good because they never missed a beat.

Flying low over the Sahara gave us a bonus of an excellent view of the remains of the ferocious desert fighting that had taken place. Burned out tanks, crashed aircraft, and every imaginable kind of wrecked equipment, both theirs and ours, were strewn all over the desert. The thought came to my mind that a lot of money could be made some day by an enterprising scrap dealer. Tons of scrap metal lay there in testimony to those brave souls that had so recently given their all in valiant efforts. It was quite a memorial sight, and I feel privileged to have viewed it.

The winds subsided, the sandy air cleared up, the time passed by and my favorite time of day came about. It was almost sundown as we approached Cairo, Egypt, and I could hardly believe that I was about to spend time in such a storybook place. The "Land of the Pharaohs." I was really here!

21

As we turned into the landing pattern, I could see the beauty of the setting sun, casting its redness onto the sands of the ages, and then in just moments as we turned onto our final approach, the jewel-like carpet of Cairo's magical lights took over the darkness. One more happy landing, thanks to my Angel's caring attention.

Chapter Nine

Our fantastic three days spent in Cairo remain tattooed on my memory. If only there was a way to actually utter a secret word that would place you back into the locale and the time you so desired. However, recall is possible and even though second best, I treasure it as my way to relive the wonderful moments of my very fortunate life.

On our first morning in Egypt, I paid a visit to the air base's flight surgeon. I had developed stuffiness in my head, and I wanted to ward off a cold if at all possible. A head cold can block your ear passages and cause pain on descent to lower altitudes. Upon examination, I received some ear drops, some kind of pills, and a wonderful surprise. Guess what? It was a three day grounding! Can you imagine, we had been ordered to remain in Cairo for three days! I wonder if the Cairo flight surgeon was perchance a relative of the Bear Field Chaplain? Regardless, they both did us a fantastically good turn.

"I can't believe I am really here."

Believe me, we knew how to not waste those three days. A Red Cross tour of the pyramids and the Sphinx, day and evening shopping trips, and general tourist activities made our time well spent.

Just being in Cairo was worthwhile. The English Hotel we stayed in made me feel as if I was somehow playing in an imaginary movie. While sitting and waiting in the hotel lobby, a couple of news journalists introduced themselves, and as it turned out, they were interested in knowing if we had any war stories of the time we spent in Eastern theaters. We told them to stick around so we could fill them in on our return, as we hadn't been there yet.

All good things come to an end and even if it's just a change to some other good thing, you gotta get up and get going. That's what we did. At night, per orders, we droned into the black sky and set our course onto the first leg of a kind of mysterious tour that would take us over lands of unknown knowledge.

Our heading was approximately N.N.E. for a while and then we were to head more easterly and follow a route that would pretty much keep us above a pipeline running through the northern section of Saudi Arabia. We understood that the populace beneath us in that area would be friendlier if we had to go down in an emergency, perish the thought.

When we got to the point of course change into the east, I took note that on the ground the lights to the north of us were in the position of Bethlehem. What a thrill that was, even though all that could be seen were points of light on the blanket of darkness. I banked our craft onto the new course and watched Bethlehem slip away from our port wingtip.

Uneventful hours passed until we landed, briefly, at the airfield in Abadan, to top our fuel tanks. For some reason, which I do not now remember, we were to make haste in our fueling procedures and get the hell out of there, and that is exactly what we did.

Our heading continued eastward, going farther and farther around this old world of ours, destination now being Karachi, which was then a city of India. You know, the first sight I still remember seeing in India was a turban-wearing man, sitting cross-legged in front of a basket with a cobra being charmed by the music of the flute. There was no question then about where we were.

The next important happening in our trip of all trips was our arrival in Agra, India, the city containing the fabulous Taj Mahal. We wouldn't have time then to visit the Taj, but certainly we would work it in later if at all possible. But Agra contained another important visit that I simply had to carry out. Through correspondence, I believed that I knew that a very good boyhood friend of mine was stationed near the famous Taj Mahal, and I couldn't wait to find out if I was right. A quick visit to headquarters confirmed my belief, and before much time passed, Vern and I were together with the entire conversation going "lickety split." Boy, was he surprised to see me, as he had no idea where I was. This was a very strange and wonderful event. The quote, "It's a small world," couldn't be more apropos.

Now I had two reasons to return to Agra, and I vowed that I would find a way. I can tell you ahead of time that the opportunity did present itself at a later date. When orders came down for a period of Rest and Relaxation, or R&R as it was known, I chose to spend it in Agra. The two of us had a few very happy days, a million miles from home!

Tearing myself away from Agra, I got back to business with my crew and our flying machine, and our mission to report for duty with the 315th troop carrier squadron, 443rd Group, 10th Air Force at Ledo, Assam, India. We took off and did just that.

Christmas card that tipped me off
to the location of my boyhood friend.

Chapter Ten

After a number of exciting hours, we were reaching the culmination of our adventurous halfway flight around the world. I say exciting because this was the big moment we had been heading for. The time we would reach the place of our action in the "Big Show" of World War II, our home, for how long we wouldn't know, but it could possibly be the place where we might be tested and maybe for our very lives. Yes, this moment was exciting.

In the landing pattern we could see that our airfield was a single landing strip with a bamboo covered tower, parking area for lots of aircraft like ours, maintenance buildings, and up a hill was an area of tents that must be where we would soon be quartered. All of this was in a cleared-out area of hilly jungle with a mountain range not very far away. I gave my last call to the tower saying, "Giggle Victor 623 — on the final approach." We were home in our new home.

Bamboo-covered tower at Ledo, Assam, India Airfield.

Chapter Eleven

T he Bear Field, Indiana Chaplain not only did us a good favor by keeping us out of the hellish European invasion, but he set us up time-wise so that we were included with the crews to be sent to the C.B.I., which proved to be the most interesting theater in World War II. Hardly anyone, then or now, ever heard of the place. But that's all right. It was a place with a big job that had to be done, and I for one enjoyed it.

Some people have heard about General "Vinegar Joe" Stillwell, and a few even remember his ill-fated campaign in the jungles of Burma. It ended up with the Japanese chasing him and his men all the way back to the border, with a threat to invade India.

Somehow the British and Americans got together with fresh forces, turned the tide around, and then mostly the Americans drove the Japanese back through the jungles and bamboo forests. That's when the crew of 623 arrived on the scene.

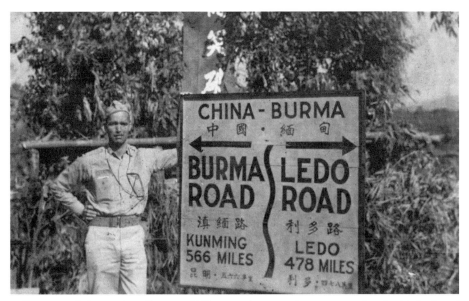

Our 443rd Group Intelligence Officer at the opening ceremonies for Ledo Road and Burma Road.

The crowd is applauding someone driving through.

Driving distances, in miles, all the way to Kunming.

"BRASS"- General Chenault, Lord Mountbatten, and General Sun.

Commemorative sign in both English and Chinese.

Chinese Dignitaries and troops.

Getting ready for first drive on "Ledo Road."

My head out of the co-pilot's window for a chance of a photograph.

I'm sure glad that we were to fly over the terrain and not walk over it. I say "walk." Actually the troops in most cases had to cut their way through with machetes if they weren't lucky enough to be able to follow jungle trails.

The part I played in the China-Burma-India theater of war proved to be the high point of my life. I was really only a kid, I think, but I did a job and did it well. Why I was doing what I was doing, instead of all the dirty, bloody, unthinkable chores that so many found themselves into, for what must have seemed like forever and a day, I will never know! I joke that the reason is God has a job for me and is saving it, and keeping me in good condition for it. I wonder what it is that I'm to do? The truth is, I have felt so blessed over and over for the times that I have survived, and whatever God wants me to do, I'll be happy to do.

Becoming a part of the 315th Troop Carrier Squadron was a pleasure. What a fine bunch of guys I was privileged to live and work with! I know that the rest of my crew must have felt the same way. Upon reporting, we were split up and assigned to wherever we were most needed. At first this seemed strange, as we had become a rather close-knit unit of our own. But of course, the newness lasted only a short while and the whole squadron was a relatively small organization. We were bumping into each other all the time.

The 315th was headed up by Colonel Love, an ex-American Airlines pilot, and I must say, a finer man was never born.

The first, next, and all the days following were busy, busy, busy. In a short time we had to get to know everything about the job that we were to become experts at. Our stateside training had to be polished until it glistened. This was our on-the-job training.

Our duties were to include air dropping supplies by parapack, carrying of cargo of all kinds, carrying passengers, and maintaining regular hospital flight service for returning of the wounded. When airdrops were planned, preparations were made in advance so we usually knew something about them ahead of time. Details of most other flights were learned at briefing just before we got to the airplane that was assigned to us for the day. What we were going to have as cargo could be a real surprise, such as goats, or anything else you can imagine. A load of pipe for the aviation gasoline pipeline that was being installed from India to Kunming, China could just about fill up the cargo bay, so we would have to pull ourselves on top of the pipes all the way from the cargo door to the cockpit. Cement mixers and all kinds of machines were on the list. Even small trucks were taken apart or cut apart and put back together upon arrival.

Air strip in Panghkam, Burma.

Airstrip in Mong Mkak, Burma.

Airstrip in Kwitu, Burma.

33

Airstrip in Managale, Burma.

I really never cared what they loaded on my plane. If it had to fly, it flew. But my one concern was how much did it all weigh? The fancy procedures of determining load weight and dispersal were cut short by necessity, I assumed, and experience and eyeballing got the job done. And a good job was always done, I guess. At least I never got to the end of the runway with my wheels still rolling on the concrete. I must say though that many times I took a good look and a deep breath at the same time.

Where we were and the kind of work we performed had to be the best and most interesting in the whole Air Corps at that time is what I say. No boredom, as every day was different. The scenery couldn't be beat, and when we got back to home base, even though tired, good food waited for us cooked by, I'll bet, the best cooks in the services. And we saw to it that they had good supplies to work with. Our return flights from China somehow usually had fresh eggs stowed on board, and a fresh meat run to and back from Calcutta was managed on a regular basis.

Our quarters consisted of large tents on concrete bases, with plenty of room for six of us, and even though the weather included a real monsoon season when the rain could seem to be solid water, we were "snug as a bug in a rug." On a clear day, from our tent flap I could see the snow-covered Himalayas way off in the distance. What a place!

One of my tent mates had a pet monkey. Cute little guy, and he must have liked us because he lived with us on a voluntary basis. He had no cage, no leash, and ran the area free as a bird...or as a monkey anyway. The only disruptive thing that he did was to perch high in the tent while eating a banana, and then throw the well-aimed peel at one of us. I wish that I could remember the name we gave him, but I can't.

Me and my bearer, Buck.

Another important member of our tent group was a young local Indian boy. He was probably about twelve years old and had been hired, along with many boys, for the purpose of providing us with housekeeping help. They were called "bearers," spending each day in our vicinity, performing various chores and paid by us on a regular basis. A rupee was an Indian coin worth about thirty cents, and we collectively saw to it that a proper number of rupees were gladly given to our

Buck and his Christmas present for us.

loyal employee. I'm sure that he felt well paid, as we liked him and appreciated all that he did from shining our boots to picking up after our banana-peel throwing monkey. Our bearer's name was Hara Sanka Achaga (I'm spelling it phonetically), and we chose to call him Buck. We really grew to love him as "our boy."

Buck's interest in our tales of what America was really like brought about many hours of important conversation, and Buck's ability with English made it easy and very pleasant. Christmas time brought unending stories of our magical season and customs to enrich Buck's already fertile imagination. This all culminated in surprise Christmas gifts that we had ready for our Buck. But the biggest surprise of all was for us. Buck had made a figure of Jesus with his own hands that he presented to his new American friends as his Christmas gift to us. Wow! It was indeed a Merry Christmas.

Chapter Twelve

B ut now, back to the business of our part in the war being carried on in the China-Burma-India theater: Our part occurred every third day of the calendar, as we were scheduled to fly one day on and two days off. As schedules go, they were made to be broken as need be, but on the whole they could mostly be counted on.

The two-day rest was welcomed after the energetic before-dawn-to-dusk-and beyond day in the air, with inclement weather, enemy pressures, cargo problems, and timing difficulties. This very active flight day could go by the numbers with no surprises, or more likely include a variety of happenings to deal with.

Weather predictions in that part of the world and at that time of our lives were less than a sure thing by a long shot. So it would not be a great surprise to have a beautiful day deteriorate into flying-on-instruments conditions.

Also a peaceful day could be shattered by the words, "Red Alert!" crackling in your headset. "Red Alert!" over the radio meant to us that enemy planes could be in our area, and if there was the possibility of Zeros meeting up with us, we needed to take evasive action without delay. Being in unarmed aircraft meant that our only weapons on board were our Colt 45s, which we each carried, although they might as well have been slingshots. Our evasive action consisted of a quickly controlled dive toward the treetops. The lower we could safely fly, the safer we would be from the threat of being shot down by Japanese fighter aircraft. Their high speed flight would require them to dive on us in order to hit our slower flying aircraft, but our low altitude would then cause them to dive into the ground if they didn't pull up soon enough. Thus, they couldn't get a good bead on us, and we were safely able to thumb our noses at them. Of course, a fair amount of luck had to be present so that they would be picked up by our radar, giving us a warning in time. Surprise could be deadly as we would then be in the "sitting duck" category.

Speaking of sitting ducks brings to mind a situation I found myself in, along with my crew and a crew of "air drop kickers" as they were called.

We were on a drop mission with six or eight other troop carrier C-47s. The place was a hilly area alongside a large flat plain that spread out to the east. We were flying over China and not very far from the Burmese border. American troops, Merrill's Marauders, were on the ground advancing toward the Japanese forces. Flying above and rather busy, I couldn't see individual soldiers, but equipment and artillery could be plainly picked out. Also the puffs of white smoke from artillery shells stood out dramatically.

Our whole group of planes was flying in a circle like "follow the leader." I don't know which one was the leader, either in front of us or in back of us, but I do know that I was very busy keeping in my place and incidentally keeping us in the air. This kind of operation requires certain techniques like no other. You fly with your cargo door off; the whole cargo bay is stacked full of parapacks; the three or four "kickers" move the fully loaded parapacks as needed. You fly the plane at about ninety miles an hour, which seems like almost stalling for a three-point landing. You have your landing gear down for added stability, your engines roaring to maintain altitude and air speed. You keep the ground markers in sight so that you can fly over the target, and when the "kickers" kick the pack out they let you know with a light signal on the instrument panel so you can turn out of the straight target approach and go around for another drop.

As the pack left the plane, the attached line would snap the parachute release so that the chute would open and hopefully float the supplies down to our waiting troops. I found out on landing back at our field that some of the packs drifted across the valley and were received by the Japanese that were positioned there. I hope they liked our American grub.

Needless to say, I felt relief when the last pack was kicked and I could get the hell out of there. I didn't know how lucky we were to get the hell out of there until a few days later when I heard of an ill-fated drop by part of another squadron at the same location on the very next day.

Japanese Zeros had come up the river valley, flying low under our radar, and shot down seven of the C-47s making the drop just like we had the day before. There is something to be said about being in the right place at the right time. (I wonder if my Angel had anything to do with our timing?)

Chapter Thirteen

Just straight cargo runs were usually what we called "milk runs" and would be a nice day's work with good conversations among pleasant people on the ground. Also passenger runs usually were uneventful, and I found very few crabby people on board.

I drew the hospital run about once a month when I was lucky. I say lucky because I got to fly a beautiful, sparkling white C-47 with beautiful nurses on board. What more could you ask for? And then when we picked up our wounded passengers for their flights to the general hospital at our base that was probably the first stop on their way home, I had a very rewarding feeling. I did wish that I could make that flight every day.

As wartime pushed on, Merrill's Marauders pushed the Japanese farther and farther south, and we found ourselves flying farther and farther south right along with them. I would land in the morning at an advanced airstrip and hear the stories of the night before. Stories of Japanese patrols in the jungle not too far from our positions; then I could hear the whining roar of a Thunderbolt P-47 diving not too far away, and then the Whoooompf!!! And the black smoke of a napalm bomb. What a way to start a day! How good it seemed to get into the cockpit, turn the engines over, and take off, always sorry for the good guys I left back there on that forlorn landing strip.

On the trips into South Burma, it seemed wise to be aware of the possible danger of enemy aircraft, so I used the training I had gained from my primary flight instructor, T. Myrle Kitchens. Remember the low flying I told you about in the open cockpit Stearman PT-17? He showed me how to roll one wheel on the road and watch out for trees and telephone poles at the same time. Buzzing barns and cattle was fun at the time, but became a lifesaving talent on the Burma side of the globe. When you were flying that low, the enemy at altitude didn't have much of a chance to spot you. We called it "contour flying," up over the high spots and down into the low spots. It was sure to keep you awake!

Winding up our day back at the base was usually a real pleasure. First stop upon landing was the Flight Surgeon's office where a stiff shot of "combat whiskey" (as it was called), waited for each of us. Then after a short debriefing, showers, the mess hall, the club or card games, awaited our attention in whatever order we so desired. Two day's relaxation was on the ticket, and we were ready to start now!

The bunch that I found myself with most of the time loved to play bridge and pinochle for hours at a time, with usually the same players. The different thing about our games was the fact that we never played for money. The scorecard was satisfying enough, and we liked it that way. Overseas card playing pots were notorious, and it was quite a sight to see the big poker games going on right after payday with all the money piled in the middle of the table, before being raked in by one winner or another. I'm sure that we had just as much fun with no bad feelings and few arguments.

I remember one bridge game that carried on one evening, with a new fourth in the place of a regular who had bought it that afternoon. He and his crew had flown into a mountain with a load of pipe on board. No survivors. We had decided to continue the game, and it was probably a good thing that we did. It was a very toned-down game, with little joking and broke up rather early.

Chapter Fourteen

My time spent with the 315th had to be about the best time of my life. Young, interesting, adventurous, rewarding, fulfilling, and worthwhile times were spent while performing duty for my beloved country at a time when we all were needed so badly. World War II had so many interesting stories on my side of the world I could write a book about it, and I guess that's what I'm doing. But I guess I should stick to my original idea of telling about the many unexplainable occurrences that have happened in my lifetime, seemingly for the purpose of keeping me well, happy and alive. Coincidence is not the word for it. I have joked about it many times, saying that God must have a job for me to do, as my reason for being here at this time and He wants me to be alive and in good condition so that I might carry out the job. Gosh! It must be some big job! Maybe with some awesome twist of fate I'm going to bring about world peace. I'd like that, but don't expect it. All joking aside, during much of my time spent here on Earth, I have wondered about the reason for my existence. Maybe I'll find out one of these days.

Up to this point in my writing there have been eight beautiful examples of God's altering the conclusion of happenings in my life and in the lives of those around me.

1.   The tailspin that corrected itself after I'd given up.
2.   Safe landing with an engine on fire.
3.   Order change from Europe to C.B.I.
4.   Avoiding the toolbox on the runway in the Azores.
5.   Safe flight through Atlas Mountain storms.
6.   Hole in clouds for contact landing at Tunis.
7.   Safe flight through that Sahara Desert sand storm.
8.   Safe completion of an airdrop with seven planes shot down on the next day at the same location.

I have become convinced that my Angel has been with me through thick and thin.

Also, I know that she is a beautiful blonde, as I can't picture some guy (even as an angel) being with me all the time. How do I rate having an angel? I don't know, but there is certainly enough need for angels in this world today. Anyway, I'm not going to question God's reason for things. I'm just happy to be included in His plans.

Chapter Fifteen

Further on during my duty with the 315th Troop Carrier Squadron, I got the call in orders to participate in a flight to Kunming, China. This was the famous run over "The Hump," famous for the relatively dangerous weather, altitudes, cold and mountainous terrain. I was excited at the prospect of making the flight but then secretly relieved with the word that the flight had been canceled due to weather predictions. (Let me tell you why I'm putting this happening in my angel list as number 9.)

Some time afterward, my original co-pilot who had faithfully flown with us on our half-way-around-the-world flight, received the same call to fly "The Hump," and he did. But on his return from Kunming, his plane, a C-46, developed engine trouble over The Hump during a blinding snowstorm. He was carrying a load of Chinese soldiers as passengers, and I think you can begin to see the extreme difficulties that were beginning to pile up.

As there was no possibility of making a forced landing, crash landing or not, bailing out was the only choice. Our guys could speak no Chinese, and the other guys could speak no English. So some form of sign language had to do. Somehow they all readied themselves with chutes and the cargo door off. All their parachute cords were snapped to the cable that ran the length of the fuselage ceiling so that the chutes would automatically open as the cords tightened after they jumped clear of the plane.

One by one they left through the open door into the cold slipstream and rushing snow. That is, until one Chinese soldier, poor soul that he was, pulled his rip-cord before he got out of the plane. You can imagine the picture in that crowded airplane.

The parachute exploded out of the pack on his back, and he didn't know what to do– neither did anyone else for a moment or two–until someone of the crew gathered up the loose parachute, put it into the hapless soldier's arms, and pushed him out the door. What else! All the others, soldiers and crew, followed.

The crew, led by my former co-pilot, made it and managed to walk out. I do not know how! A lot of the details were lost as I got the story second hand. But I imagine that there were a number of angels on board that day. I pray that there were enough angels for all the Chinese soldiers.

Chapter Sixteen

Flights followed card games, and card games followed flights. Months followed months, and seemingly endless chains of blessed letters flew back and forth between home and the jungles. What would we have done without those letters?

I feel so fortunate to have so many colorful memories that I can call up into daydreams and view them with my mind's eye. Some may continue for quite awhile, and others might be just random flashes of scenes. I'm the projectionist in my mental movie theater, so I run the show any way I want to. I'm having a lot of fun showing the films that I'm viewing for all this writing. Should have done it a long time ago, but I guess everything has its time and place.

Some random shots that I have just seen while writing this portion include:

- Looking out my cockpit window and seeing a rather large wrench lying balanced between two cylinders of my port engine. It remained there for the rest of the flight and didn't fall into the path of the propeller blades. (I'm going to call this incident number 10, because we sure would have crashed into the jungle if that wrench had done a job on my port side prop!);
- At night, looking way down where the jungle carpeted the scene and seeing red tracers of machine guns firing into our direction, friendly fire and far enough away to look pretty in the darkness while not being dangerous;
- Looking ahead into the morning fog and low-hanging damp clouds, while letting down during a mail run flight and finally seeing the wanted air strip through the swirling mists so the letters could be delivered to our guys;
- Looking out across the night sky with a large moon low enough to be included in the picture of fairly close popcorn-like cumulus clouds, intermittently lit up with internal flashes of lightning;

- Looking out at the sunsets the world over. What a wonder of the mind to be blessed with!

A whole touching story of the last hour of a late afternoon mission flashes across my mind's eye. We were flying fairly low, following the river into southern Burma, with our eyes intently searching the left riverbank for a white marker that would identify the target we were looking for. Our last parapack on board was to be dropped at that location and then we could head for home.

My crew chief, peering over our shoulders, was first to spot the white marker up ahead on our left. With eager shouts we all got ready to wind up the mission and go home. I gave our man on the ground a radio call, to which he replied, and soon our pack of goodies was floating down to him. He acknowledged our accurate drop of needed supplies with a firm "thank you." I replied with a "Merry Christmas," as it was Christmas Eve. Our un-named friend on the ground answered with a cheery, "And I wish you a very Merry Christmas." The silence that followed and the darkness that closed in on us as we climbed for altitude and our heading home was unbroken for awhile. We all felt a tearful pang as we left our friend in the dark on a night like this.

Chapter Seventeen

With a shivering chill, a whole series of pictures sweep through my mind. Pictures of a return flight from Burma during late afternoon many, many missions after our arrival in the C.B.I. so long ago. It had been a sort of odds and ends kind of day. We had dropped off a variety of pieces of cargo to a number of airstrips and along the way replaced cargo with a variety of military passengers holding orders for transit to Ledo and points beyond. A sunny and pleasant day was being replaced with a sky full of tall cumulus clouds. It wasn't a threatening scene, but just a lot of it; nothing to do but maintain a safe altitude and fly on instruments most of the time.

A late afternoon slipped into "sundown time," the surrounding mists of clouds took on an eerie reddish hue that was disconcerting to say the least. It seemed kind of like flying through a weak mixture of tomato soup, a very unnatural setting.

The lateness of the stressful day, topped off with instrument flying through a tomato soup sky, brought on a disoriented condition known as vertigo, which I had experienced before, but certainly didn't welcome at a time like this. We had all been trained to believe our instruments no matter how we felt we were flying. But it's mighty weird to feel like you are climbing or diving or hanging one wing down, when your instruments show that you are straight and level. My co-pilot for the day was a Warrant Officer glider pilot, a good, well-trained pilot but in a theater with no gliders. He was filling in and doing a good job, even though a little light with experience. Joe spelled me a lot at the controls, but I naturally took the bulk of the responsibility no matter how I felt.

Back in the cabin our free-loading passengers became concerned after not seeing anything but red mist. After a short time the ranking passenger, a general, became somewhat of a pest by visiting the cockpit too many times with too many questions until I convinced him that we were very busy and should not be bothered.

With time going by, the redness outside of our bird slipped into darkness which was a lot better. Altitude, heading and time were the important facts to be concerned with as we had to clear the approaching mountain range before we could safely let down to a lower altitude in welcome home territory. Every once in a while, through a nicely placed hole in the clouds, lights on the ground could be seen which were recognized to be headlights of a convoy of trucks winding their way along the Ledo Road. This verified our position on course for home.

Soon the mountain heights were behind us and we could let down into the flat plains where ground lights pinpointed the scene. But you know, after being in a blind condition for so long, the little lights and the dark black terrain were confusing and nothing looked familiar even though we'd flown over it many, many times before this. After welcomed words of advice from friendly voices in our tower, all of a sudden the ground and the lights began to make sense and we knew we were almost home. The runway lights looked as good as Broadway in New York City.

With wheels down and locked, we were in the landing pattern, parallel to that beautiful runway, then on to the base leg and then onto the final approach . . . but then I could feel it was wrong. We were too high!

 With the engines cut back, we had too much speed. We were too high and coming in too "hot." We were settling, but I knew that our wheels wouldn't touch until we had used up half the runway. Now the runway looked like it really was a comparatively short jungle airstrip that required touchdown to be near the beginning edge so most of the remainder could be used for braking...we were too high...we couldn't make it...that big old tree way off the end of the runway was shining white in the brightness of my landing lights...why had I misjudged my speed and height so much? "Gear up!" I hollered, and Joe didn't waste a second. The gear whined up as the engines roared with the throttles wide open...we were flying...was that white shiny tree too high? We were climbing out of the field, but it all seemed like a slow motion moving picture. The tree...AHHHH!!!...it was under us, not by much, but it was not out of the picture. I think that I must have been holding my breath for a long time, but now it was great to breathe again. I slowly gained altitude and came around to another landing pattern for another try. But who was I trying to kid? I had had it!

Like the time, long, long ago, when I almost spun into the ground, I felt weak and was sweating bullets. But unlike that time, the side vent window was already open with not near enough cool air coming in and besides that, I had a co-pilot this time…"Joe, are you okay to land this thing for me?"

"Sure," was his quick reply.

AMEN!

Joe made a nice and welcome landing. Thank you, Joe…Thanks, Angel!

Chapter Eighteen

A short walk on good old terra firma carried my weary body to Squadron Operations for debriefing and my free "Combat Whiskey" that I felt I had earned this time. Another short walk carried me to our club, with our bar and with a few portions of my favorite scotch and soda. I do believe that I bypassed dinner that night. At least, I don't have any memory of dinner, for some reason or another.

Morning came with a completely different mood and a healthy appetite for bacon and eggs, and a bottomless coffee cup. It also came with a message from Colonel Love, my Squadron Commander and my favorite pilot. So, with no delay after breakfast, I hotfooted it over to operations with quite a few questions in mind as to the reason for the call.

It really came as no big surprise to me that the colonel wanted to talk to me. After all, I knew that I had blown it on the last landing. Also, ever since my flying cadet days, I knew what the answer was when asked the question, "Why?" after doing something wrong. It had been burned into my memory that the only acceptable answer was "No excuse, Sir." And my landing attempt was a bad one! In fact, I only had God to thank for not killing us all during those dark minutes. It was one more Angel Pearl strung on a beautiful string of events that were adding up in my blessings.

Colonel Love listened to my account of the day and evening flight with interest and understanding. His quiet acceptance of my factual narration was a welcome surprise to me as I knew that it could have been different. Instead, he said he thought I had reached a point of stress that called for a change of duty. As I didn't have quite enough time in combat action to qualify for rotation back to the States, he put me in for transfer to a Liaison Squadron.

Colonel Love explained that the 5th Liaison Squadron flew single engine Stinson two seater aircraft. They were based in Bhamo, Burma, and had been doing a lot of observation work for ground troops and artillery spotting. Being a different kind of flying, he thought I might like the change. I also would have a chance to build up some more flying time so I could qualify for a trip to stateside.

Me pretending to be a Republic Thunderbolt pilot. "Anything for a photograph."

Me and my L-5 at Bhamo, Burma.

"Get OUT of my Jeep!

If I decided to take the transfer, he said he would have a liaison pilot come to Ledo, acquaint me with the aircraft, check me out as Liaison Pilot, and the transfer could proceed. Without a moment's hesitation I said, "Yes." What a break for me! Instead of receiving a reprimand, I was given a wonderful opportunity.

The plane came to Ledo. I flew it. I loved it. I transferred to Bhamo. I started a new chapter in my Book of Life.

The light airplane flying in the mountains was so different and so much fun. Mostly I flew VIP passengers and mail runs to all different kinds of locations. On the ground, I was made the Squadron Transportation Officer, which was really in name only, as the non-coms (non-commissioned officers) knew exactly what they were doing and didn't need me to butt in. But I did get my own jeep along with the title.

Getting my own jeep reminds me of another interesting little story. One evening, instead of going to our squadron mess hall, I decided to go to the Officer's Club at the main airfield in Bhamo in order to have a kind of special evening and dinner. As the parking lot was rather full, I parked some distance from the club entrance and made my way into the friendly environment.

It's magical how a few hours of dining in pleasant surroundings with music and friendly conversation can take the edge off the war and the jungle. You can almost forget you are on the other side of the world, but then reality creeps into the scene and it's time to go.

When I stepped out into the parking lot, I was struck by the darkness and emptiness. Most of the vehicles were gone, and I could hardly see my jeep off to one side all by itself. As I drew closer, my pace slowed down with the alarming feeling of apprehension that swept over me. The darkness hid from my sight what my intuition told me. It told me that there were others near me in the quiet, and probably in my jeep. A couple of steps further and I could then see into the shadows, that what I felt was right. Three Chinese soldiers were quietly sitting in my jeep. Without a moment's hesitation, I began to holler orders to them to get out of my jeep. I didn't know if they understood English. I didn't know if they were armed. I didn't know if they were going to kill me for keys. I didn't know what to do except to keep up what I had instinctively started to do. As I kept hollering at them to get out of my jeep, I stamped around them like I was the toughest officer they had ever run across. And you know what? It worked! They all slowly got out and just stood there while I jumped into the driver's seat with the key magically in my hand and into the ignition. The engine's roar spun the wonderful little jeep out of there, and you can bet I didn't look back.

All the way back to the squadron my mind flipped over the possibilities of what could have happened. We were probably all armed. They might have been drunk. Who knows? But I do know now that I can score one more for my Angel. Bless her. I just know that my Angel must be a girl angel, and she is probably the most beautiful angel that has ever existed! Wow! What can I say about all this? I guess there just are not enough proper words at my disposal to express my feelings. I'll leave it at that.

Chapter Nineteen

With the exception of Chinese soldiers in the dark, my duty with the 5th Liaison Squadron was a great change of pace. Good weather, with a good airplane to fly and with comparatively no pressure, proved to be an ideal way to wind up a successful tour of overseas duty.

My mind's eye can see so many little sections of happenings while stationed at Bhamo, Burma. They are almost like moving snapshots. I'll try to put them down in words .....

Late one afternoon, when the Magic Color Hours occurred, as the lowering sun gave everything a golden glow, I was waiting at a small airstrip in a place called Katha, Burma. A vehicle was to meet me to receive a packet of documents.

While waiting, a beautiful Burmese gal approached alongside my aircraft. I can still see her colorful gown and immaculate white, lace-trimmed blouse. After greetings and some small talk in perfect English, her musically toned voice invited me to have tea with her. Talk about

Airstrip at katha, Burma, where I turned down an invitation for "tea."

My Bhamo bearer heating water.

Chopping wood to stay in shape.

Doing my laundry.

temptation! While listening to her soft words, I was conscious of a back-drop of scenery. It was a single file of saffron-clad monks descending a narrow path to the bottom of a hillside. What a picture! Needless to say, my polite "No" saved me from a court-martial for dereliction of duty.

One day while off duty, my buddy and I drove to meet a Burmese lady that we had heard of. Her business was trading in precious stones and jade. After all, we had to bring some pretty baubles back with us from the Orient!

We found our lady, and she took us to a nice grassy spot where we all sat down on the ground around a white cloth that she had spread out. She then produced several leather pouches and spilled out a dazzling array of gems and jade. Our eyes must have popped like saucers, but soon we recovered and enjoyed the bargaining. Not able to speak much English, she passed a piece of paper back and forth, first with her high figure on it, and then with our low figure. Gradually the figures came close and the deal was made.

We had fun, ending up with some nice pieces. We might have bought some bargains, and we might have been taken on some, but it was a pleasant way to spend an afternoon on a hilltop in Burma.

One sunny morning while flying over mountainous terrain with a VIP passenger in the rear seat, I was enjoying a few hours of relaxed duty. Our destination was Dr. Seagraves' hospital at Namkam, Burma. The noted doctor was none other than the "Burma Surgeon," famous the world over. My VIP passenger was General Sun, a powerful and high-ranking commander in the Chinese army. Our flight was uneventful up to a point. That point was when I realized my first flight to Namkam was confusing and I was not sure of my location. The General picked up on my searching gaze out to the left and then to the right. The General's "not speaking much English," and my zero knowledge of Chinese, left us with sign language for our system of communication. He had a chart of some kind and was trying to help, but of course I was on my own.

What seemed to me to be a long time was probably not much at all. However, I was sweating out the possibility of being hopelessly lost with a Chinese general on board. Imagine the relief I felt when I regained my orientation. It also was a pleasure to see the General's smile after a smooth landing on the hospital's airstrip.

How's about a snapshot of a military wedding? How's about a snapshot of a secret flight to spirit away a prospective bride from her Air Force headquarters to a secret location in the jungle? How's about secret

Me and my 5th Liaison Squadron

romance in spite of World War and Brass Objections? I must confess my part in the secret goings on hinted at in the above questions.

A fine and popular pilot in our squadron fell in love with a wonderful and beautiful nurse stationed at a not too far away military hospital. In seeking help for a possible wedding to take place before our pilot's transfer to China, only opposition and lack of understanding prevailed at the top of the brass ladder.

Lucky for the situation, a group of us imaginative friends of the loving couple decided to act heroically, and also, we thought it would be a lot of fun to thumb our noses at authority.

Each of us took one part of the plan and went to work. My voluntary part was to sign out an aircraft; land at the bride's closest airfield; sneak her away to the secret jungle airstrip; and thus deliver the bride to her waiting groom.

All the pieces of the clandestine plot fit together perfectly, providing a successful and beautiful wedding ceremony with bride, groom, best man, maid of honor, chaplain, music, rice, audience and reception with all the trimmings. Thankfully for us, we got away with it all, without the brass knowing anything about it. Some luck!

Chapter Twenty

Some time after our Jungle Wedding, the wonderful news of V.E. Day (Victory in Europe Day) was heard on all of our radios and soon was followed by the official word. This meant that all emphasis would be placed on the anti-Japanese action, and we could have more hope of the war ending and our going home.

My good fortune caught up with me when I received word that I had built up enough time for rotation stateside. The fantastic picture of a quick flight home seemed real at first as my Operations Officer efficiently processed my orders. I was to proceed to Calcutta and then home via Rome, Paris and New York. Wonderful! But then the "old game" was played and my silver 1st Lieutenant's bars were bumped by the gold of a Major. My quick flight was transformed into a two-month wait in Calcutta for passage on a general class ocean transport vessel, which proved to be 65 days all through the Pacific.

Admiring "art," or whatever her name was.

The above turned out to be not too bad after I got over the disappointment of not being able to hurry home. Calcutta was an interesting place to hang out, as long as I was fortunate enough to know a friend who had been transferred from my old 315th Troop Carrier Squadron to Air Force Headquarters. Joe said, "Come on and stay in my place. I've got plenty of room." I did and enjoyed the two months greatly. The food was good, the Officer's Club was magnificent, and we even had entertainment during the dinner meals. Can you imagine the entertainment included singing by Tony Martin, who was a sergeant based at 10th Air Force Headquarters. There were also a lot of

Directing traffic in the shade.

Burning ghats in Calcutta. This body is ready to be burned.

Fire has just been lit.

Holy Man in Calcutta street.

pretty girls to look at. Good place!

When the happy day came along, and I and scads of other happy guys and gals boarded our homeward bound ship, we breathed a sigh of relief, not knowing that we would be spending the next 65 days with the Navy. Of course, I had no complaints really, as the Officer's quarters were quite nice and a free Pacific cruise wasn't going to be complained about.

You might ask, "Why did it take 65 days to cross the Pacific?" Well, that's quite a story, which I will relate to you now. Details of how I made it from 10th Air Force Headquarters to the dock alongside a huge General Class Navy Transport are lost in the dim memory of the past, but I do recall the thrill of seeing my transportation home for the first time. It was quite a sight, and the wonderful feeling kept getting better and better as the minutes and hours ticked on and on.

With the blast of the big ship's horns and the gentle feeling of movement, we all knew that we were finally homeward bound. Then soon the confined port waters became open ocean waters, and we were well on our way in the Indian Ocean, first stop Colombo, Ceylon.

It didn't take many days to become seasoned ocean travelers, especially speaking for those of us who didn't get seasick. I was one of the lucky ones and thoroughly enjoyed the motions of the ship on the high seas. Then too, when the weather turned rough, it meant that there was more room in the dining area for those of us that still had an appetite. I never knew what the percentage was for the unfortunate seasickers, but it must have been quite high.

My home for 65 days while at sea.

The joke passed around among us straight and level pilots was that it was mostly hotshot fighter pilots that couldn't take the motion of the waves, and I do believe it was true. I don't remember if they ever seemed to get over their digestive difficulties.

Chapter Twenty-One

After Ceylon we did some serious voyaging all the way to Australia. Weather was great, sunsets spectacular, porpoises fun to watch, even saw a whale spout. But the big, big happening came about as our destroyer escorts began blowing their horns and whistles and were soon joined by our ship's horns. Rushing out on deck to find out what all the noise was about, we all soon knew the news that an atom bomb had been dropped on Japan. What excitement! Strange how so many bottles of secret booze could all of a sudden appear. Like magic, celebration was in order. Then before making port in Perth, Australia, we got news of the second bomb being dropped.

By the time we all went ashore, the news of Japan's surrender had broken, and we Americans were greeted in town with open arms. You would think that our money was no good. Everything was on the house! What a fantastic three days we spent in Australia! You bet we didn't want to leave when the time came, but we did. However, an Aussie band on the dock saw us off with "Waltzing Matilda" that we could still hear when they were almost out of sight.

A long time after "Waltzing Matilda," while proceeding on an easterly course paralleling the southern coast of Australia, and during the dark of night, all hell seemed to break loose. It turned out that it was a Granddaddy of all storms that our Captain had been warned about, but he had decided to head into it anyway instead of delaying our departure by a day.

My bunk was a good one. It had railings to hang onto so I wouldn't be thrown out of bed. However, I found myself hanging on to keep from beating my head against the steel bars. I certainly couldn't sleep, so I dressed and roamed around to see what was going on.

Soon I found something very interesting to watch through a glass panel in a bulkhead, looking into an operating room in the hospital section. Apparently a sailor with appendicitis was having an emergency operation. It would have to be an emergency because no one in his right mind would pick a time like that for surgery if it weren't necessary. Everyone including the patient was held in place somehow to keep from being thrown around the room. How they ever managed to cut the right things with the ship being banged around the way it was, I'll never know. I could hardly stand and hang onto a railing to satisfy my curiosity. However, I did check on the sailor's condition the next day and was happy to find out he was doing fine, thanks to everybody's skill and devotion to duty.

Another thing happened that night, and it pointed up the severity of the storm. With all the noise and banging throughout most of the night, I can't say with which bang it happened, but a monstrous wave action actually bent the bow of the mighty ocean going vessel so that in the daylight it looked as if we had collided head on into an immovable structure. Wow! I guess we were fortunate to get through that night as well as we did. My Angel must have had a lot of help on duty with her.

Our next major change of course was to the north, passing by the eastern coast of Australia and heading for New Guinea. This heading now started a lot of serious discussions, arguments, predictions, and anything else you can call the talk among all of us involved passengers. We had begun our happy voyage during World War II with the planned destination being the USA, after first unloading all the general hospital personnel on board at Okinawa. However, now with the Big War over, what were they going to do with all the hospital people? It was probably a sixty-four dollar question for somebody, somewhere, to answer. In the meantime, we were all floating around the Pacific, but still heading in the general direction of Okinawa.

Our next port of call was Hollandia, New Guinea, where we spent a couple of days acting like tourists on a cruise. Sightseeing and shopping for souvenirs was not bad duty and easy to get used to. Next we sailed through the Philippine Islands, not stopping, but getting a good look close up, of a lot of half sunk warships of all kinds. You could just picture MacArthur wading through the surf and onto the beach.

Chapter Twenty-Two

Our arrival at Okinawa was certainly different. The approach to the harbor took us well within sight of the shore, where our naval forces were in action against the Japanese who were still holed up in caves along the beach and rocky shore. Evidently they weren't going to surrender, so we were shelling the cave entrances and using napalm. It was an ugly sight and it all seemed so unnecessary. The war should be over for everybody.

We anchored in the harbor rather than docking. As no word was said about shore leave, we assumed that it would be available later. But we were wrong! The next day it was announced that bad weather was bearing down on us. It was a typhoon and all the ships were ordered out of the harbor. They were to form a typhoon formation and all proceed in the same direction and at the same speed so as to prevent collisions. Radio communications and radar were to be maintained, as sight could be impaired.

Our ship prepared to get underway without delay. The speedy but quiet action of our crew reflected the seriousness of the situation. The mood was catching, and I felt the tightness of breathing and a desire to get to a high point so that I could see the approach of the monster. However, my curiosity was not strong enough to dare me out on deck, exposed to harm's way. Instead, I just remained in a patient composure wondering what the coming experience would be like and feeling glad that our ship was as large as it was. Just imagine the fear that would be present for the poor soul in the same position but in a small vessel. I can't conceive the feeling.

Before long the typhoon hit and it was impressive. The movies could never capture the excitement of the real thing, no matter how good were the "special effects." Being on the ocean at that time carried the experience to the heights. I have run out of words.

We were at sea, maintaining the formation, for a total of three days. The people running the show knew what they were doing, and as a result, there was no loss of life or equipment. I can't speak for the land conditions. On shore they would not have had the marvelous control that we had.

During the storm it was difficult to keep one's self busy. Not having a job to concentrate on, time passed slowly. Everything you tried to do was tough. Finding a corner you could remain wedged into for awhile could be recommended. Walking, standing, sitting was good for only a short time and then you'd have to change. Laying down flat wasn't too bad, if you were on a soft surface and could hang on to something. I guess that was why nighttime was welcome. You were so tired that you automatically fell asleep in your own little bed, and the storm drifted away out of your consciousness.

Being trapped inside finally got to me after hours and hours groaned by, so I got brave and dared to figure out a way to feel what the outside was like. Not being a complete fool, I went to the lee side of the ship where there would be protection from the gale, and slipped out through the door, hanging on all the while.

Out of the worst of the wind and with a firm grip on the ropes strung about the deck, it wasn't too bad. However, I didn't get too adventurous either. A little way out onto the deck was enough. If that gale blowing ever had gotten hold of me, there wouldn't be any way I could have held on to the rope, no way!

I don't know how much wind speed there was out on that open water, but I do know that it had enough force to blow the surface almost flat! While I was watching the sea, a half-submerged lifeboat topped a flat blown swell. It remained in my sight for a short while, and I could see that there was no sign of life aboard. I'm glad because if I had seen a poor soul clinging to the inside of the hull and I couldn't do anything about it, the tragic picture would have remained with me forever.

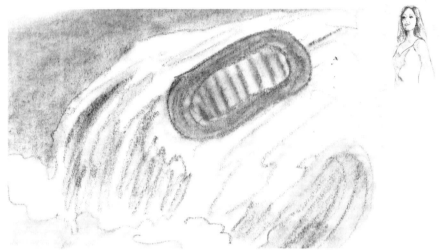

Finally I had enough and took to the safety and comparative quiet of the ship's interior. It had been good to feel and hear the might of the typhoon and be none the worse for it. Oh I did suffer some loss for my experience. My beautiful low cut boots that I had made for me in Calcutta, got wet out on deck and the salt in the leather never could be removed. They had cost only a few rupees, but I hated to have them spoiled.

Our typhoon having blown itself out, we all sailed back into the snug harbor and took a well-deserved rest for a couple of days. The reason for our being in Okinawa in the first place was to bring the general hospital to its new home. Well, you probably guessed it. Some people must have put their heads together and come up with the idea to send all those people home since they weren't needed anymore for the war effort. Hooray! So now we could all finally go home.

Chapter Twenty-Three

Going home meant that we would head in a general easterly direction and some day soon reach the West Coast of the Good Old United States of America. How wonderful that sounded! One thought that we kind of liked was that we might make one more port and stop in Pearl Harbor. Why not finish off the cruise with a bang! But it was not in the cards. Our dear captain decided on taking the great circle route, which did not get close to Diamond Head and grass skirts. Oh well, we were in a hurry to get home anyway.

Finally at home with my wife, Ginnie.

Days and nights of perfect weather took us peacefully to our home waters. After sixty-five days on board, we stood off the California coast in San Pedro Bay and waited for the morning fog to burn off. What a strange feeling it was to be almost home after so long; to have left so long ago, not really knowing if we were to live or die, or come home in one piece. Thanks to God and my Angel, I made it in good health.

After quite a long time the fog cleared, and our big ship gently docked with horns and whistles blowing in celebration. We were home!

We spent three days on a Marine base for processing and shopping for some new uniforms. Couldn't go home looking like a bum! Then a train ride across half of America, playing bridge most of the way. Arrival in Chicago, into a taxi, and home with my wife and Mom and Dad. How sweet it was!

Ginnie and me in Jamaica having happy days.

A buddy that lived not too far away had a car, and the arrangement was that he and his wife would pick up my wife and I, and we would all go together to Kellogg Field, Michigan, where we were to be separated and turned into civilians. That we did. And after several days of papers, papers, papers, and more papers, we were separated.

One of the questions on one of the sheets of paper asked if I wanted to be separated from active duty to take a reserve commission. Of course I said yes, as that is what I had programmed myself for. That was my answer, and it was some time before I questioned my wisdom.

Civilian life was different than I had remembered. I felt like I had grown up in the military, and I had loved flying. Then all of a sudden, my life was completely different. I found out that life was not just a bowl of cherries. I wasn't too happy with my decision to say yes. I tried to reverse that ye with no luck. Then I tried all the airlines for a job flying with no luck. All the bomber pilots were doing the same thing, and with a lot more four engine time than I had. I just had to make the best of it, and I did. I fashioned a good life for many a year.

Left to right: Granddaughter Sarah, Grandson Brad, Daughter-In-Law Cindy, and Son Roger. "Having happy days."

Grown-up granddaughter Sarah.

Grown-up grandson Brad.

My good life was a happy life with a happy marriage that moved from Illinois to Arizona for many more good years. They were not adventurous years, but solid family years until the day, through illness, my loving wife Ginnie, passed on. I need not elaborate on the days that followed. They were tough, but God saw me through, just like my Angel took care of me so many times against all odds.

Chapter Twenty-Four

Whoa! I'm letting the cart get in front of the horse. I almost forgot part of my story. It's true that civilian life after the war wasn't as adventurous and life threatening as I had grown accustomed to, but things did happen even then.

Some time after peace had taken over, a bunch of us from our young people's church group went to the Indiana State Dunes Park for a beach party and a fun-filled day. Of course, you can't have seven lively, young guys and gals in the water with a beach ball without a lot of action, throwing, catching, chasing, yelling, and just plain fun! The day was bright and sunny, the wind was light and pleasant. The water was cool and wavy, but we thought the waves just added to the fun, and they did. It was great!

As happens when you are in the open water and not confined in a pool, you can chase the ball here and there, and without knowing it, gradually get farther and farther out until … all of a sudden, all seven of us were out in water that was over our heads. We all realized our predicament at about the same time, and our yelling quickly changed from fun to fear, but it sounded the same to those on shore. They all thought we still were having a great time, never suspecting that we were yelling for help. Of course at this beach there were no lifeguards anyway. However, there might have been some better swimmers than were some of us. I could swim pretty well, but not really good enough for a situation like this.

When you are in the water and can't touch the bottom, it is awfully hard to keep your head out from under the water. You sink under and work your arms like the dickens to reverse your movement downwards to upwards, only to go back down again. It seemed like something was pulling my feet down, so that I couldn't get my body up horizontally on the surface of the water to swim toward the shore. And every time I did bob my head up out of the water momentarily, I could hear the others yelling. I yelled! I grabbed onto a big gulp of air; I saw my wife's red bathing cap, and I saw Chuck, who was a strong swimmer, trying to keep her head up because she could hardly swim at all. And then I'd go down again.

After awhile (I don't have any idea how long), I got so tired and had so little strength left, I just seemed to stay down there where it was quiet and the world looked kind of all green. There was just a kind of bubbly sound in the water. I didn't really think any thoughts, and I didn't see my life pass before my eyes, but I guess I did know that I had had it. It was so quiet and peaceful …but all of a sudden both of my feet touched the sandy bottom at the same time. I gave a mighty push and shot up out of the water like a surfacing submarine! How impossibly wonderful to see us all walking out fairly close together.

We probably all swallowed some water. I know that I did. In fact, I was spitting up some little chunks and pieces of wooden debris for some time. My wife had taken in a lot of water and was in a bad way for quite a long time. But we all were alive and kicking. Thanks to God!

I don't remember who it was that noticed a strange fact about the scene before us. When we looked out at the great expanse of Lake Michigan that we had just walked out of, the waves were coming from the right side of the picture as we saw it. Yet we knew that when we were having so much fun in the water, and when we were about to drown in the water, the waves were coming from the left side of the picture. The difference in direction had to be about 90 degrees. We must have been taken out to deeper water by an undertow and then pushed back in by the change of direction of the waves. Kind of spooky, isn't it? But then, when I think about all of my life's happenings, it just all fits in real nice. Thank you, my dear Angel. I wish I knew your name. Maybe some day I will, but until then I'll just call you Angel. Come to think of it, how could I think of a more beautiful name?

Chapter Twenty-Five

Please excuse the little jump backward in my life's narration. I just couldn't leave out such a lot of excitement, especially since we all survived the watery experience.

Speaking again of water leads me into the next phase of my adventurous days in this lifetime. After Ginnie passed into her next adventure, my days just piled into a string of day after day after day. We had moved our life into Arizona and loved every minute of it. Now seen through just my eyes alone, it looked quite different and not so interesting. Our home was so empty, and the quiet was deafening. One of our friends, I can't remember who, said, "You'll just have to make a new life for yourself." After giving it some thought, I decided that it was a piece of good advice, so I acted on it.

The "Ginnie Lee"

All my life, water had been very special to me in any way I found it. Rivers, lakes, oceans, stormy or not, all were full of magic and lured my imagination into their direction.

Water calls for a flotation device of some kind. So to pursue the subject, I got out the Yellow Pages and, "let my fingers do the walking," starting with the letter B for boats. Living in the desert, I didn't expect much, but surprise! I did find a boat dealer and started from there. After a short drive, I was in the shop among the many kayaks, canoes, inflatable rafts, etc. I never had a whole lot of experience as a sailor, but just enough to always yearn for more. Now I seemed to be getting closer to more experience.

There! I was seeing just the right boat for me. It was an eight-foot sailing dinghy, sparkling white with a beautiful blue sail. Absolutely the most perfect vessel for launching my new life that I could possibly find. It was a deal.

It should come as no surprise that my new sailboat would take on my late wife's beautiful name and become the "Ginnie Lee." I spared her the possibility of structural damage by deciding not to break a bottle of cham-

The "Ginnie Lee"

pagne over her bow, but instead chose a more simple ceremony while painting her name lovingly on her hull.

Very little time was lost in the rush to get her into the water. Outfitting and planning were put aside, and even the wait for more ideal weather was skipped. The Ginnie Lee fit into the truck bed of my yellow pick-up, so off we went to the closest Arizona water, Lake Patagonia. With just the power of oars and muscle, we made our short but triumphant maiden voyage, with wind and spray under a dull and threatening sky. However, we were spared rain and the day turned out to be a great success.

"Ginnie Lee" turned out to be a perfect trainer and brought back the familiar feeling of good seamanship. I took every advantage of free time and good small-boat weather, because it's important to match your boat's limitations to the weather, especially when you have no heavy keel and your light hull bobs about like a cork.

In a light breeze, there is no finer experience than slipping silently along over the sparkling ripples. Going along at about the same speed as the breeze, you feel no movement of air, even though your sail is full. It's magical, as if you have the power within yourself. But don't let the magic lull you into day-dream-land, as I did.

I was dreaming along on a warm, sunny afternoon, powered by the silent, magical breeze. Peacefulness was everywhere at that moment. WHAM! The boom swung violently from portside to starboard, and the sail filled with the new strong wind with a crack that could be heard quite some distance, I'll bet. As the sail filled with new air, the boat filled with water, pouring in over the now submerged starboard side. I had been minding the tiller from my cushioned center seat before all the action, but now found myself going overboard headfirst, with nothing to grab onto but air. I saw in kind of slow motion the lake cascading into my boat. But then, all of a sudden it changed, and I was sitting back in the center with all of my possessions floating in a boat half full of water. I remember how funny it looked to see one shoe float by me.

The big emergency was over, but the big wind still "doth blow," so I had work to do. The sail had to be lowered and the boat had to be bailed out before I had time to think. But when that time came and I thought about what had just happened, I knew why it had happened. I was simply caught flat-footed while I was daydreaming.

If I had been alert, I would have seen the change in the water surface. You can see that a long way before it gets to you. That's the "why" answer. But the big unanswered question was "How did I get back in the boat?"

You tell me. I was going overboard with nothing to grab onto, but all of a sudden I was back in the center, looking at my boat half filled with water!

I know you probably won't believe me, but I am absolutely convinced that my Angel has been taking care of me for all these years, for why I don't know. Maybe it's her job. I'm glad if it is, but why me? Why should I be favored in this way? These are some big questions I feel will be answered when I cross over to the other side.

Chapter Twenty-Six

M y pretty little boat did so much to change my life's pace and direction. She showed me that there was a real side to my many years of adventurous fantasies. Always I desired to put myself into the heady stories of the sea. You know that, inside your mind, if the desire is great enough, you can smell the scents and feel the wind and spray on your skin, without ever believing that some day the desire could become reality.

My pretty little boat helped me to step out of my grief without ever having to lose a single thing. I could have a new life, and all the beautiful memories of the past, both at the same time.

Many sailing pleasures followed one after the other until I knew that I was hooked. However, I needed a bit more boat to help along my transformation into a real sailor. A 14-foot "Sunfish" that I found proved to be just the right thing. More sail, more mast, more new details to master, more happy days on the water aboard my bright yellow sailboat, "Ginnie Lee II."

The "Ginnie Lee II"

The "Ginnie Lee II"

My new boat had her own trailer to ride on from home to surf and back again. And "home" for her was a protected spot in a friend's rental lot. My sailing routine was taking on a serious look, and the look was not the only serious part of the developments.

Dreams of sailing had always included my living on board and traveling to distant ports of call. Stories of "single handed" around the world

The "Ginnie Lee III" ready to take on the world flying my son's flag
—well he is a "Jolly Roger."

had always taken my breath away. Does all this sound laughable? Maybe plans beginning to get out of hand? Well, I never did get out of control, but I could see that there should be practical ways of bringing my fantasies to life. So I began to plan my sailing adventure in a down to earth way.

Brad and I talking things over.

I couldn't afford to have two homes, one on land and one on water, so I'd have to sell my house. And of course, the money would help out, to say the least. My boat would have to be big enough, but not too big. My possessions that didn't have anything to do with my planning would have to be disposed of, as there was no reason or place for storing. These thoughts had many more thoughts attached, but are too many to detail.

Serious efforts, one after the other, brought about my ownership of a perfect sloop, the "Ginnie Lee III." Without doing another thing, I had just about fulfilled my dreams. But after a few days of pinching myself to make sure I was awake, I went to work and real work it was.

Chapter Twenty-Seven

My grandiose visions of a single-handed, around the world voyage had simmered down somewhat but still remained rather ambitious. The plan, simply stated, was to remain in the Great Lakes around and about Holland, Michigan, where I had found my "dream boat," until the approach of autumn and cold weather. Then I would set out for Chicago, the waterway to the Mississippi, and down the river routes to the Gulf of Mexico, timing my arrival to miss the last of the hurricanes. Spring would find me off the East Coast, sailing for New York and the entrance back into the Great Lakes for the summer. With luck, I intended to never put my gaze on snow again. Snow is pretty, but I had seen enough of it to last me for the rest of my life.

To get ready for the day that I would set sail on the beginning of my big adventure would take a lot of time and concentration, so my trips in and out of Holland were not too many. Only the need for more supplies and an occasional special dinner, such as a big steak, lured me away from my boat. The rest of the time found me tied up in the slip, working and planning on board, or out sailing on the lake. When in town, the hours spent were extremely enjoyable and worthwhile as the people there couldn't be nicer. Help and friendship was all around. I do miss Holland, Michigan, a lot.

Finally, one early morning, when all the details had been thought of and taken care of, the sunrise cast its welcome warmth on Ginnie Lee III and me in the cockpit. The feeling you get when you take the wheel for the first time, alone, with the heading out of port for your first destination, is indescribable. I felt as tall as the skipper of a nuclear submarine. My sailing adventure had begun.

My planned course was simple. I would proceed off the Lake Michigan coast at the south end of the vast body of water, destination the Chicago area. Not being an "Old Salt" with all kinds of experience, I chose not to test myself. Each day that promised good weather found Ginnie Lee III enroute to the next scheduled port. I found the port to have desirable facilities, and distance to cover, was just enough to fit into a relaxed morning's passage. If I did a good job of planning and the weather forecasts were correct, and if I agreed with the experts, there would be no surprises. Usually we all agreed.

Port after port offered a friendly stay, and upon tying up at Michigan City there was no real reason to feel that there would be any break in the string of smooth sailings. Not being overly superstitious, I didn't place any importance in several rough occurrences during our arrival at the Michigan City Marina.

First my usual radio call to announce my intended entrance into port within fifteen minutes remained unanswered after a half dozen calls. Finally a brief answer was received, with no directions for entry into an unfamiliar port. Having no choice, I stood off the entrance until finally receiving the limited directions. However, upon entry through a comparatively narrow space in a high stonewall, I realized that the directions were confusing and almost caused me to blunder into a shallow section. A man's frantic waving me off was the only thing that saved Ginnie Lee III from being mired in the mud.

After a bit of time, better directions sent me in the proper manner to an empty slip for a safe tie-up. But wait…don't count your chickens until they hatch!

On the way to that safe tie-up, an unfriendly crosswind caught us broadside in a tight spot and added to my nervous reaction of the moment, causing me to scrape the stern of a too-close moored sailboat. No damage resulted, but my frayed nerves screamed out at me, only to be covered up by the loud surprised shouts emanating from people on board the disturbed, moored sailboat. I'll bet they spilled their coffee and whatever else they were drinking. My muffled apology had to suffice, and I took my embarrassed red face out of their sight. I'm happy to say nothing else was ever heard from those unknown sailors.

Chapter Twenty-Eight

M y unhappy and difficult arrival at Michigan City Marina seemed to be a harbinger of some bad times ahead. Could my "peaches and cream" days at sea soon be over for awhile? We'll see.

After tying up in a very nice slip that was finally assigned to Ginnie Lee III and me, Michigan City Marina didn't look so bad. After a good lunch and a number of cups of good coffee, the place looked absolutely great! My intentions were to stay for two nights and then get an early start away, providing the weather held. Now a little rest and relaxation were in order.

My second day in port was leisurely spent on necessary details. The time sped by, and the weather was to hold for another day, so all was set for our next to last leg of the journey to Chicagoland.

A good night's sleep followed by corn flakes and hot coffee gave me all the energy I needed to gather my lines and smartly set sail for open waters, and then a berth in Burn's Harbor. The sky was clear and the seas were calm. It looked to be a great day ahead.

Up to now my day by day voyage had seemed usual and routine, but all of a sudden, I felt excited by the proximity of "big time" waters, with hundreds of classy yachts, fancy harbors, and huge ocean-going vessels and ore boats. The traffic would be demanding and quite different from the up to now laid back existence. Also a month-long visit with my son and his family was reason enough for a feeling of excitement.

Pleasant thoughts and pleasant weather was helping to pass the time away nicely. But, speaking of weather, what was that way up ahead? Good weather was supposed to hold at least until the next day, but it sure looked like quite a buildup of clouds on the horizon, and it was gradually increasing in stature. Becoming more than just interested, I listened to Weather and sure enough, the picture was changing with the approach of a front in the next few hours. By that time I should be snugly tied up in Burn's Harbor.

I kept watching ahead but felt secure in the knowledge that the information I had from a fellow sailor that I had talked to back in Michigan

City, was that Burn's Harbor was a large facility that should offer all the conveniences that I'd ever want.

The more I looked ahead at the weather approaching, the more I wanted to hurry up. But then we were almost there, and I was glad! As I maneuvered into a wide entranceway between two high stonewalls, I picked up my microphone to announce my position and ask for permission to enter for the purpose of obtaining a slip for the night. Before I could get out my first word, the breath was taken out of me by what I read on the high wall, portside. A large painted sign told me that the port was to be used solely by commercial craft and that no pleasure craft were allowed. This news stopped me "dead in the water."

Burn's Harbor happened to be the only facility I had no printed material on. I was going by word of mouth, and it was plain that the mouth I had been listening to didn't know what it was talking about. What a pretty kettle of fish I was in! An approaching storm with a fairly low tank of diesel, and the only way to go was back to where I had just come from. Well, at least I didn't have to spend any time trying to make up my mind. There was no choice; I swung around with a snappy one eighty and tried not to look over my shoulder for a little while.

When I did look back at the approaching weather, it was still there of course. No magic had made it disappear, and naturally my concern made the picture all the uglier.

I had felt secure with my fuel supply as the distance involved would have been no problem. My thought of topping off my tank with diesel had been canceled by a malfunctioning pump at the fuel dock. Instead, topping would be done at Burn's Harbor. Oh yeah! Well, the only thing to do was to let the Coast Guard know of my predicament, which I did. Their reply was they would monitor the situation Ginnie Lee III was in and come to our aid if necessary. That knowledge was reassuring to say the least.

Time went by like watching and waiting for a kettle to boil. Nothing is slower! However, the storm in the rear quadrant wasn't slow. It looked like it was speeding along, trying to catch us. Continuous glancing back at the ominous sight did no good, but it was impossible not to look. My gaze seemed to constantly bounce from my watch to my compass to my fuel gauge to my rear view of the storm and back all over again. Everything seemed to remain about the same, except the time on my watch and the approaching look of the following storm. It did look like it was catching up on us, and it certainly did look like it was getting uglier.

The fuel gauge on my diesel tank was a float type with a red mark that showed how much fuel there was. If it would remain still, the amount left would be more easily known. But with the action when underway, there was a lot of bouncing and guessing. However, if there was a bounce you at least knew there was some fuel left. As if that was any consolation!

Radio weather reporting was no comfort at all. Each time the details grew more alarming, with taller waves and stronger winds. Thank heavens there was still quite a bit of calm water to look at between the storm and us. I wished that I could see how much was left between Michigan City and us.

I have never been much of a whiz at computers and the like, and as a result, my GPS personal navigator was lying in the bottom of my ditty bag, and I couldn't ask it how far we had to go for an end to all this concern. Right then and there I promised to learn how to use the handy new gadget, even if someone had to pound the info into my head. I was just hoping the big black storm cloud wouldn't catch us before I had another chance to learn.

More looks to the rear confirmed that we still had a chance, and my diesel continued to sound strong and reliable. The time had passed at the proper rate, and my educated guess was that we would make it, even though I knew it would be close.

As the front grew nearer, it seemed that its approach was picking up speed. It probably just seemed that way, but the wind was increasing and the dark sky seemed to be almost covering us. The storm's size was so huge it threatened to swallow up everything in its way. Ginnie Lee III and my entire world were insignificant in comparison.

With the first feeling of cold drops of moisture hitting my skin, I sighted the harbor's stone storm breaker jutting out beyond a protruding peninsula. It seemed to be fast approaching and couldn't have been prettier for my money.

As we rounded the storm breaker, the rain came down in earnest. Our timing was perfect, and our tie-up was completed. We were soaking wet, Ginnie Lee III and me. I stopped at the Coast Guard station and conveyed my thanks for their watch, and at the marina office I made arrangements for our stay until good weather.

Next morning I filled my diesel tank and noted that it was almost dry. My dear Angel must have been hovering nearby while we were sweating it out. I will never take her for granted, and will always be grateful to the bottom of my soul.

Chapter Twenty-Nine

The great big bad storm that chased us for miles and miles proved to be just that...a great big bad storm. It must have been angry that it got cheated out of the chance to rough us up, and I can't say that I'm sorry for that. When it hit Michigan City, after we were safely docked, the fury of it lasted throughout the night. The rain, gloom and high seas lasted the rest of the week.

I looked at the gray sky and I looked at the crashing waves spraying over the storm breakers until I was sick of it. Weather report after weather report all sounded the same, like a broken record playing over and over.

Michigan City Marina is a really fine place, but rather far away from the city proper. Without my own transportation, day-by-day existence got to be a bore. Also, one restaurant within walking distance was not enough for a whole week, even though it was a very nice one. The fact that it was usually raining while walking to and from didn't help. One day a nice guy, I think he was the manager of the marina, offered me a lift to a grocery store for supplies after he heard me asking for directions. He even came back to pick me up while I was waiting for a bus. A really nice guy!

Being stuck in a place for a long time with no activity of importance makes it necessary to improvise ways of passing the days and nights. When not reading, writing letters, playing solitaire, or napping, many hours of serious thinking occurred. At this time in life I wasn't filled with concerns for the future, as I felt content with what I saw. But looking at past happenings during recent years brought feelings of thankfulness and much wonderment mixed with awe. Who am I to be able to walk through so many experiences of life, brushing past harm and death as if favored? I credit my Angel, partly with tongue-in-cheek, but mostly with thanks to God. It's hard for me to believe that I am writing all this about me. I just shake my head in disbelief that it is really I.

Chapter Thirty

Finally, after all my patience was almost used up, the United States Weather Bureau came through with what might be great news. They claimed that five and a half days of rain and wind and high waves would end come sundown, with two-foot waves and diminishing swells by midnight. They predicted a window of about twenty-four hours for clear skies, low waves and low swells. By the next day another storm was to move in and spread to the east, but all the way to Chicago was to remain great weather for at least two days. So it was all systems go for my passage to Chicago.

Lucky for me, that evening allowed me about six hours sleep with no disturbances, so when my alarm sounded at three a.m., I could bound into action. With preparations taken care of in advance, I was ready to shove off by four. The sky was black with millions of stars shining through, the air was chill and damp, and still no roar of waves crashing against the storm barriers indicated that the reports were right and the seas had calmed down a good deal.

Ginnie Lee III's red, green and white running lights looked pretty in the darkness, and the low, strong tone of her diesel was a welcome sound in the vast quiet. I untied and pulled in my last lines. With a little throttle, we backed out into the black water and then we slid forward, and we were underway. What a beautiful, free feeling!

We passed all the quietly sleeping boats on our way out to the open waters. Then with a turn of the wheel, we headed into the dark loneliness of the great Lake Michigan.

Leaving the still harbor water behind, we now felt the lively action of deep water. The low waves passed with a little rushing sound and the low swells slid under our hull with a rolling quiet. The rigging sound of fittings clicking and clacking gently against each other on the mast seemed to be keeping time with the water's movements. All these sounds fit together into a musical composition that only I was hearing, because this was really alone, me and the stars. But I must say, those quiet stars were sure beautiful.

Rounding the massive storm breakwater, we headed toward Chicago. This time we would go all the way and not even slow down when we passed Burn's Harbor. Boy, that name gives me the willies every time I think of it. What an experience! But I did learn a good lesson, not to take someone's word without checking it out.

As we headed for the big city, I could faintly see a hint of a glow on the horizon in that direction. With passing time, the glow strengthened into brightness of light, and then the light gradually took shape. In fact, three shapes were very slowly rising out of the distant water. They were distinctly separated into what all of a sudden I realized were the Sears Tower, the Standard Oil Building, and the John Hancock Building. They were ablaze with light and seemed to be all-alone sticking up out of the water. What a sight to see!

As more time circled the face of my watch, the three pillars of light became attached by ground lights, and then the whole string of coastal lights floated into sight, up and over the horizon's edge.

The coming of dawn gradually took over the distant light scene and I could no longer watch the approach of my destination, but I knew it was there. What a beautiful world this is, and I am glad that I have been so privileged to be able to see so much of it.

The next big event on the program was sunrise, and it was an event; just enough wispy clouds to pick up delicate pink to gold color from the glorious sun. It rose with all the majestic promise of another good day.

Now, when we came into the proximity of Burn's Harbor, I could relax and give it a wide berth. In fact, I steered well out from the coast, as there were a number of giant ore carrier ships and ocean going freighters standing off shore, waiting their turn to enter with their cargoes.

While the scene of my not-so-happy, frightening experience dropped below the horizon in the rear, the happy shores of days to come were getting nearer and nearer with every rising swell. I could hardly wait for the few hours to pass until I'd be able to see and join with my beloved family.

It seemed to be ages since I was last with my son Roger, my daughter-in-law Cindy, my granddaughter Sarah, and my grandson Brad. The life of a sailboat sailor is one of patience and steadfast endurance, without the need or desire for the blinding speed of the powerboat advocate. However, with the approach of the coming meeting and greeting, I felt the wish for a high-speed engine and the ability to put it on the step to eat up the distance that remained. Instead, I sat back and relaxed and enjoyed the thoughts of happy days to come. We were all to be together for most of the month of August.

Finally the harbor of Hammond Marina was in sight, and I was standing at the wheel with eyes searching for the first glimpse of some loved ones. Certainly some of them would be awaiting my arrival. After all, I had been away at sea for a long time. I looked and looked and looked. Then, hooray!. There they were! Cindy, Sarah, and Brad all waving like mad, from a walk on the top of the breakwater. I felt like the returning hero from some great novel, and all the efforts expended had been worth it.

Soon, with the excellent directions that had been supplied by Roger, I found the slip that Ginnie Lee III was to use, thanks to Roger's good friends. Then hurried docking and flinging of lines brought hugs and kisses and laughs and shouts and unleashed happiness. How great!

Chapter Thirty-One

For the next three weeks plus, my stay with family was more like a home-coming than just a traveler's stopover. We talked and talked; we visited and visited; we dined and dined; and really enjoyed being together during the time we had.

Besides having fun, I used the opportunity to pick up a few items I would need or want in the months ahead. I also called on a few friends that I hadn't seen in a long time, and tried to satisfy all their curiosities about my travels and my experiences while living aboard my boat. Then there was the necessity of fitting my vessel for river passage, as my mast and sails had to come down and be stowed. Many of the bridges I would pass under would be too low.

Ginnie Lee III was built for single-handed operation, even for the lowering of the mast. However, since I was new at this sort of thing, I thought it better that I enlist some more muscle, just in case. Brad and a young friend of his were more than willing to help. On a sunny, calm day, we managed the job and enjoyed doing it.

As it always happens, time flies when you are having fun, and we were having fun, and I don't know where all the time went. It seemed like only yesterday that I sailed within sight of Cindy and the kids waving their arms off at my arrival, but here it was, almost time to leave.

The weather was to be good the next day. Evening was upon us and we had all bid our fond farewells, some tearfully. It was time to take leave, so Roger drove me to the marina. After another hug and a "Hasta La Vista," we parted.

Alone again. Gee, I had really become so used to having a gang around me, it seemed strange to be in the quiet all of a sudden. But I guessed it wouldn't take too much to get used to the single life again. A quick check to make certain that all things were ready for the early morning departure. The alarm was set, I was tired. I was fast asleep.

Radio alarm is a wonderful thing. It's so much better to waken with soft music in your ear than the jangle of an old-fashioned alarm clock. I was up and zipping around, with everything done and all shipshape in no time at all. The sun was just up too, and it was a glorious morning to be alive.

Before you could say "Jack Robinson" (I wonder where that saying came from?), the diesel was purring, the lines were stowed, and we were once again sliding out of the slip.

As we passed the fuel dock, I remembered the almost empty tank back at Michigan City and was grateful that Brad and I had topped the tank the day before. It was a lesson well learned. The forecast for good weather had been right, and as we passed the breakwater and turned out into the deep, nothing could be seen but sparkling waters and not a swell in sight.

A counter clockwise turn of the wheel, our bow swinging to port side, and we were heading for the mouth of the waterway that would carry us through the countryside of the state of Illinois to the Mississippi River.

Ahead was a completely new experience! The tales of river traffic and dangers of huge barges by the hundreds, and what to do and not to do while traversing the many locks were enough to make your hair stand on end. But I had decided I could manage, and I did. I'll admit though, it was all a thrill I will never forget.

Chapter Thirty-Two

Upon reaching the mouth of the Illinois Waterway, I took a deep breath and turned into it. I was the only moving vessel to be seen and it all seemed eerie and quiet. In fact, it was some time before I saw a living soul or another moving vessel of any kind. But then I spotted the familiar sight of a speedboat coming my way. He was cutting right along, heading for the open water of Lake Michigan. As he got closer he thoughtfully throttled down so as not to cause too much wake on passing. We exchanged customary waves and smiles, and then the whole world seemed more relaxed and friendly.

My diesel pushed me along as I steered through the unfamiliar channel, checking the depth all the way. I figured there was plenty of water under Ginnie Lee III, but I wasn't about to take anything for granted. Also, I had been warned that submerged logs could be a hazard. So I guess the rule of the day should be "keep on your toes." I did, and stayed out of trouble.

With no troubles coming about, time went on and the miles passed steadily under my keel. Rounding a gentle bend in the channel, I caught sight of my first train of barges. It was only three in line and they were tied up at a dock, but they were big! I could just imagine the frightening size of six of them in pairs being pushed by a diesel boat in my direction! When they would be real and not in my imagination, I would have to concentrate on not being scared into shallow water, trying to stay away from the monster. Being left grounded wouldn't be a picnic either.

Hours ticked away and the ever-changing scenery passed by. The channel banks at first were dominated by factories, piers, docks, and huge storage tanks of all kinds. Nothing was pretty, and I'd say everything was pretty ugly, and all covered with various shades of dust and dirt. The tourist trade never visited this part of the world, I'm sure, and I was glad to see that it did not go on forever. Thankfully, it finally gave way to a more rural look. The weeds and scrub gradually changed into bushes, grasses and trees, and then into real countryside. What a welcome change!

Most of the morning was past and very little traffic had shown itself. Several pleasure craft leisurely went by in both directions. One speed boat with an idiot at the controls tore past like a rocket, with a wake that smashed side to side in that narrow channel so violently I had to hang on and couldn't even let go my grip enough to shake my fist at him. Oh well.

I was just regaining my composure from the wake episode when I finally saw barges galore bearing down on me from ahead. I say bearing down on me because that is what it looked like to my inexperienced eyes. Actually, it was a paired line of four barges on each side, making a total of eight being pushed by a most powerful diesel boat. They were well to my port side with a lot of room between us. But I wonder how much room to spare there would be for me if two paired barge columns were passing each other going both ways. Of course, I don't really want to care about how much room there would be. I wouldn't want to be mixed up in that no how!

As the big diesel boat passed me, I could see the captain on the bridge as he waved to me. I felt a thrill, being acknowledged by the captain of such a powerful vessel, as I waved back. Gee, this was a friendly place after all, and I liked being a part of it.

Chapter Thirty-three

According to my chart, I was not too far from our berth for the night, a marina that I had phoned in advance. This procedure was very important whenever possible as they could say at the last minute that they were full and you would be left with no tie-up for the night. I'd hate to be on the water all night with no anchorage or tie-up, as the barges run twenty-four hours around the clock. What a nightmare that would be!

There was just one more thing between Ginnie Lee III and the marina for the night. It was the first lock that we would go through. As I sighted the lock's structure ahead, I took another deep breath, same as I had done upon entering the mouth of the big waterway. I always sweat out big and new things that I'm faced with. It's just my way, so this was one more to face. I knew what to do, but it was the first time and I don't like making mistakes. So I radioed ahead, asking permission to enter the lock. Replied permission was granted almost immediately, along with explicit instructions, including that I was to wait for a green light as a signal to enter the lock.

When the time was right, I saw the green light flash on and I proceeded. The Lock Master had directed the boats entering to remain close to the lock wall on our starboard side. The other three boats did that as directed, but I had a problem. My mast, boom and wrapped sails were lashed to the starboard side, making it impossible to work from that side. My radio explanation proved to be enough, and permission was granted to use my port side against the other wall, as both walls had ropes hanging from the top.

I took up my position, halfway into the lock on the side to my left. A few minutes later, the Lock Master came to a position on the top of the wall, close to me but a little above. He politely asked if I was alone on board. When I replied in the affirmative, he explained that I would still have to handle two ropes at the same time in order to keep my boat parallel with the wall. One rope for the bow and one for the stern. This I could do, standing midship with my arms stretched out to left and right, and not having to worry about my hull scraping the wall as I had hung four fenders on the port side.

Slightly nervous, I waited for something to happen. I knew that a lot of water had to be emptied from the lock in order to bring us down to the level necessary for us to sail out of the lock when the forward gate would be opened. Then the first thing began to happen. Almost silently, the gate we had just passed on entering began to slowly swing shut. When completely closed, I noticed that we were very slowly lowering our position relative to the lock's wall and the ropes were slipping through my hands. There was no real turbulence, just quiet. I had imagined all kinds of action, but that was not the case.

I didn't time the procedure, but it did take quite a long time to empty all the water necessary to drop us some forty feet. When the level was reached, the forward gate began to slowly and quietly swing open.

With the changing of the signal light from red to green, we all slowly proceeded on our way without having to stop at a tollgate. Just think, all that service for free. Of course, we pay taxes, but it still seems pretty nice when you think about it.

Chapter Thirty-Three

According to my chart, I was not too far from our berth for the night, a marina that I had phoned in advance. This procedure was very important whenever possible as they could say at the last minute that they were full and you would be left with no tie-up for the night. I'd hate to be on the water all night with no anchorage or tie-up, as the barges run twenty-four hours around the clock. What a nightmare that would be!

There was just one more thing between Ginnie Lee III and the marina for the night. It was the first lock that we would go through. As I sighted the lock's structure ahead, I took another deep breath, same as I had done upon entering the mouth of the big waterway. I always sweat out big and new things that I'm faced with. It's just my way, so this was one more to face. I knew what to do, but it was the first time and I don't like making mistakes. So I radioed ahead, asking permission to enter the lock. Replied permission was granted almost immediately, along with explicit instructions, including that I was to wait for a green light as a signal to enter the lock.

When the time was right, I saw the green light flash on and I proceeded. The Lock Master had directed the boats entering to remain close to the lock wall on our starboard side. The other three boats did that as directed, but I had a problem. My mast, boom and wrapped sails were lashed to the starboard side, making it impossible to work from that side. My radio explanation proved to be enough, and permission was granted to use my port side against the other wall, as both walls had ropes hanging from the top.

I took up my position, halfway into the lock on the side to my left. A few minutes later, the Lock Master came to a position on the top of the wall, close to me but a little above. He politely asked if I was alone on board. When I replied in the affirmative, he explained that I would still have to handle two ropes at the same time in order to keep my boat parallel with the wall. One rope for the bow and one for the stern. This I could do, standing midship with my arms stretched out to left and right, and not having to worry about my hull scraping the wall as I had hung four fenders on the port side.

Slightly nervous, I waited for something to happen. I knew that a lot of water had to be emptied from the lock in order to bring us down to the level necessary for us to sail out of the lock when the forward gate would be opened. Then the first thing began to happen. Almost silently, the gate we had just passed on entering began to slowly swing shut. When completely closed, I noticed that we were very slowly lowering our position relative to the lock's wall and the ropes were slipping through my hands. There was no real turbulence, just quiet. I had imagined all kinds of action, but that was not the case.

I didn't time the procedure, but it did take quite a long time to empty all the water necessary to drop us some forty feet. When the level was reached, the forward gate began to slowly and quietly swing open.

With the changing of the signal light from red to green, we all slowly proceeded on our way without having to stop at a tollgate. Just think, all that service for free. Of course, we pay taxes, but it still seems pretty nice when you think about it.

Chapter Thirty-Four

Being closer to the open gates, we were first out of the lock, soon to be passed by the others. Their friendly waves wished us well. Then once again, all the scenery belonged only to us. My boat and I were the masters of our destiny and watched over by God and Angel. Quite a group!

Just a few minutes out of the lock, I was glad that my lock companions were far out of sight so they didn't witness the unseaman-like predicament I found myself in. Nothing too bad, except that poor Ginnie Lee III was a prisoner of the only seaweed around, and there was a lot of it. We were stuck, just like in the mud. Backward and forward was out of the question, so I did the only thing I knew how to do. That was to sit back and calmly think my way out of my troubles.

From what I could see, we had just barely stumbled into the large patch of weeds, and if I could somehow clear the stringy stuff out from under our hull and around the three-bladed propeller, we could carefully reverse out of the mess. It would only take work, so with time and patience and the boat hook and lots of sweat, we finally slowly reversed until we were clear and free.

How nice it was to be able to continue on our way once again. Not too much time had been lost, but I was anxious to get to our mooring for the night. Every bend in the channel held promise for sighting the marina. When it was not there, the feeling of disappointment could not be helped.

Finally as we rounded another curve, there it was. Not much to look at, but it sure looked good to me. A few frame buildings in back of a docking area, with a dozen or so slips. Some had boats in them and some were empty. I headed for a convenient empty slip and easily came to rest in it with a sigh of relief. I was tired, hungry, and stressed from my first experience with barges, locks and seaweed.

The closest building looked promising. It had a window facing the water, and neon lights spelled out "Smugglers Cove" and some popular beers. My bet was that inside I would find the manager, an O.K. for the slip I had taken, and some food. I won that bet and happily sat down to enjoy the beginning of the end of the first lap of the trip to the Mississippi River.

"Smugglers' Cove,"
I guess this is a good place for a skipper that flies the "Jolly Roger."

9My overnight stay turned out to be all that I had hoped for: delicious food, well-served, and very nice people to talk to. I was lucky to find everything so pleasant. It began to rain in the evening, and that caused me to decide to remain until the heavens dried out. I had several comfortable days, and if it wasn't so important to get going, I might have been tempted to stay longer. The threat of weather change with the coming of autumn was on my mind a lot. Even though I didn't have a real schedule, I had to keep ahead of the changing seasons. It was a long way to the gulf, and I had a lot of time if I didn't tarry too long.

With the promise of good weather, I called ahead for my next stop, and at the crack of dawn I was off again. The conditions remained favorable, and I made good time day after day. That is, I made good time until there was mechanical trouble at one of the locks. When I radioed for permission to use the lock, I was informed that I should stand by for further word. Well, I stood by and stood by, and when I called the Lock Master again, the information was, "Not yet, but maybe soon." Finally I was given the word that the problem had been cleared up and I could proceed into the lock with the green signal. Yeah! Hallelujah!

To an onlooker I would have appeared to be completely happy with the ability now to get moving. I was happy, but underneath there was a

Train of barges heading up the waterway.
First barge, second barge, diesel engine pushing boat.

nagging concern with the time of day as it was getting on to late afternoon. I had to get to my next point of overnight stay, and I was worried. The usual phone call had not been made as the published information said, "No telephone." Oh well, if I could make it there before dark, I'd tie up some way. If they didn't have a slip, I'd run a line to a tree and drop a stern anchor. Golly, here I am starting to talk to myself out loud. Get with it, Eastman.

On and on I dieseled until I came upon a man on the shore working on his boat. I shouted to him on passing, asking if he knew of a good place nearby where I could tie up for the night. A welcome reply came back, "Just on the other side of that bridge ahead is a place called River Club. They have docking facilities and you'll be welcome." I gave him a loud and enthusiastic, "Thanks a whole lot," and a wave. I couldn't believe my luck, but as I drew closer, I could see that it was all true. Sure enough! There was the River Club in all its beauty, complete with outside tables and chairs and pretty, colorful umbrellas. Believe me, I lost no time tying up, fore and aft, to large rings set in concrete; then a leap onto land and into the friendly atmosphere of the River Club.

My new-found port-of-call had smiling people, music from a juke box, and a lady in charge waiting to take care of her new customer's needs. She answered yes to my request for overnight tie-up, and at no charge, if you can believe that! Next thing to take care of was an order for a big steak, medium rare, with all the trimmings. It turned out to be perfectly done, and you can bet on the tip being very generous. My evening spent at the River Club was a high point on my Illinois Waterway voyage, topped off by a good night's sleep.

Chapter Thirty-Five

Sound asleep, safely docked in front of the River Club, I found myself gradually awakening and becoming aware of the noise of activity outside on the water. It still was very dark, and the air in my snug cabin was rather crisp, but I just had to slide the rear hatch open to see what was going on.

I found that the docking area on my side of the channel, but farther down stream, was lit up like Christmas. Where there was nothing but emptiness when I turned in for sleep was now a beehive of activity. But instead of bees, there were huge barges, all with lights shining from positions on sides, bows and sterns. No one would ever be able to say that they couldn't see them coming.

I could count eight of those giants that were being lashed together into a double column of four pairs. Men on the barges and diesel boats in the water were doing all the work. Everybody involved knew exactly what they were doing, and it was really a smooth running operation. I was glad, though, that my vessel was out of the way and that I had had presence of mind enough to have my navigation lights and my anchor light lit for safety sake. A collision with one of those monsters would be all she wrote.

I watched the activity with intense interest as if I was glued to the spot until all was ready for them to leave. As the sky was taking on the look of approaching dawn, an air horn signal was sounded and with surprising quiet, the whole double column began to move past Ginnie Lee III. The intensely bright searchlight atop the diesel boat's bridge kept sweeping the water ahead of the columns of barges, from bank to bank, until they all rounded a bend in the channel and were out of my sight.

Dawn was breaking. The time was just right for starting another day. I was wide-awake and ready to go, just as soon as I had some coffee and cereal. I couldn't go on an empty stomach.

The before-dawn show I had watched from the best seat in the house stayed with me all day. It was so very interesting to see such a professional performance of such a difficult job, made to look easy, because everyone involved knew just what they were doing. It would have been a good lesson for a large part of the world.

My day had started out on an up beat and continued the same way throughout the whole day and on into the next day. Problems were few and no complaints were necessary. The only thing that was lurking in the back of my mind was the knowledge that I was tired. Not physically tired, but mentally and psychologically tired. Having to be constantly on the ball with no room for error was wearing me down. Without realizing it, I was sweating out everything all day long. The water depth, floating logs, weather changes, barges around the next bend, where was the next tie-up, would they have diesel fuel where the book said they would. Those disturbing thoughts in the back of my mind grew more serious when I developed them into the whole picture of all the distance to the gulf, and then up the East Coast and back into the Great Lakes. After all, I wasn't even to the Mississippi yet!

After completing a rather difficult docking at a rundown marina that had seen a lot better days a long time ago, I gave a sigh of relief. The guidebook had said to "be careful of shallow water when docking," and the book was right. Finding deep enough channels with a cantankerous wind blowing and unreliable warning buoys had been a real problem. I was bushed. I sat down on my bunk and could have cried. That is, if I could cry! I never have cried in all my years; choked up, but never cried. I've been told that it's good for a man to cry when it's warranted; it lets the pressure out. But anyway, I never have.

Sitting there, I felt so bad to have things going that way when all my expectations had been so rosy. I really didn't know what to do. I'm not a quitter. I never have been. What to do? So, I sincerely asked God what I should do. With closed eyes and bowed head, I just sat there for how long I don't know. But I do know that when I began to move around, I knew what I had to do. I had heard no deep voice from above. I had heard nothing with my ears, but still I knew what to do. With no questions, God had let me know what, and I set out to do it.

First I called Roger and let him in on what was going on. He was shocked but supportive all the way. Next I called Don Pollard, owner of Pollard's Landing, the sailboat dealership in Holland, Michigan, where I bought Ginnie Lee III. With my words of explanation, Don said it was lucky that I called when I did as he was scheduled to leave town in a few days. He had to make a trip to pick up a new boat, but he would be able to help me. Don said when to expect him to arrive with my boat's trailer, so we could get her out of the water and back to Holland. I was elated to have the arrangements made, but felt it to be a bittersweet experience. I hated to end my glorious adventure now and in this manner.

Roger called several times after our initial conversation, checking to make sure that all arrangements were proceeding properly and that I was okay. Don was as good as his word, arriving in two days at the time he had promised. His wife came along to share the driving.

Our trip back to Holland was pleasant, uneventful, and sad for me. I honestly felt like it was the end of my world. There was no way I could rationalize to myself the ending of such an important piece of my life. What others thought didn't matter. How was I going to pick up my existence and continue, doing what? That was the inner conflict I was having. I knew conversation with Roger and those close to me would help, but right then I had to be content with just the thoughtful care and handling of details.

Back in Holland, Michigan, the starting point of my would-be adventure; it was time to get to work. Unloading my boat and deciding what stayed and what was to come with me took a couple of days. Don was to clean up the boat and ready it for sale. Roger came to get me, and with a little trailer full of my stuff, we journeyed to the Chicago area and my family's home.

Leaving Ginnie Lee III was so heart rending, it seemed to have built a block in my mind, and it's not really clear to me how it all went. I just knew that she was gone and I didn't know what I was going to do or where I would be for the rest of my life. I guess it's good that I didn't retain all my feelings during that period. It seems rather awful to me, thinking of it now. But I survived and I must have done a lot of right things because I'm fine and happy now. Life does go on!

Chapter Thirty-Six

I said that life does go on, but where? I was back in Illinois with my family, and I was trying to get used to living on dry land. But I really could have been classified as homeless. I wasn't going to stand on a busy street corner with a sign and sell newspapers. But where was I going to live? I intended to be around for a long time if I had anything to do with it, but where?

No, I wasn't about to hang around near Rog and the family. I wanted to see and be with them as much as possible, but I thought it would be better to commute. Also, I'd die if I had to put up with northern winter weather. I had been an Arizonan too long for that. You know, "100º in the shade, but it's a dry heat!" Come to think of it, the whole idea of living the year around on Ginnie Lee III was to be in warmth and sunshine. If I could not be on the water, at least I could be in the sunshine. So that was settled! I was going back to good old Arizona and be with all my friends, and commute as much as possible to be with my family.

Now that the big problem was solved, I had to get going. The spark was coming back and I was eager to do things, putting all the disappointments on the back burner. I was getting excited about going home, and I couldn't wait. Time flew and before I knew it, I was ready to hit the road. I repossessed my Chevrolet Malibu that I had given to Cindy (she didn't mind), hitched a small rental trailer on the rear with all my stuff, and was ready for the farewells. But I guess you're really never ready for good-byes. Gosh, I loved them so much, and was so full of gratitude for their loving concerns and prayers. One thing for sure, there would be no "Adios" said. It would be "Hasta la vista," because it was written on my heart that I would always return, time and time again.

Chapter Thirty-Seven

Yep, I was going home. I was on the road again with all my possessions and all my memories and all my dreams. Yes, I could still dream of things to come. Not wild adventures. Rather, I was content with the memories of adventures I had already owned. Finally, I dreamed of a life filled with relaxed living among all the things that would be every day pleasures. Friends, scenery (mountains, cacti, sunrises, sunsets…), weather (I love the Arizona monsoons with all the quick changes from sunny days to rainy storms with lightning lit skies), and then the desert flowers that come after the welcome moisture.

I had a lot to think about and to see and enjoy during the five days of leisure driving on my way back to Arizona. The gradual change of countryside from midwestern to southwestern was exciting for me. It seemed like I was away from my beloved Arizona for such a long time.

At last the days passed by and I was home. Then there was phone calls, knocking on doors, ringing doorbells, surprising people that didn't know I had returned, hours of answering questions, and hours of describing everything I had seen and felt and done. It was all just as I had believed it would be; couldn't be better.

In no time at all, I was helped by a dear friend Jamie, a realtor, to find a great little villa to hang my hat in. Don, my boatman in Holland, sold my beautiful Ginnie Lee III so I could pay for my little villa. Life was moving right along in such a nice way. I even found a good part-time job after awhile. I had retired ages ago, but really never stopped working in some way or another. Work was good and a little extra money also didn't hurt.

My part-time job as a security officer required driving back and forth to my place of employment in Tucson. Living in Green Valley, some distance away, made the drive home lengthy, and with night driving traffic problems, it was not too desirable. However, it was only a two-day, part-time job. On one of those nights, my drive home turned into a problem. My Angel had been on stand-by for a long time. My activities had been so usual and unspectacular, her only responsibility was to remain awake and not doze off. Well, things were about to change.

The night was moonless and dark, but dry. Traffic was not too heavy, but very fast, way too fast and close. Everyone seemed to be in such a hurry. On my route, the usual roadwork ahead signs had mostly been taken down. The roadwork had been going on for months, and I was so glad that the orange barrels and flags were gone. Only one section was still under construction. It was a bridge-widening project that would probably go on forever with all its orange barrels, wooden horses, flags, and anything else they could think of. The slow speed signs meant nothing of course, even with threats of big bucks in speeding tickets. Once in a while a squad car with rotating lights did the job.

The night in mention had no officer, no patrol car, and no rotating red, white and blue lights. As I drew closer to the bridge construction, the lanes had been narrowed down to a single lane, but traffic was still too fast. I kept hitting my brakes as a signal for the guy in back of me to slow down. The red signals had to be screaming to him as he kept tailgating, "Get off my tail! Get off my tail!" My headlights bouncing off the too-close orange barrels were blinding but I could see in the lane ahead a dark, stalled car, with no way around it. Not only was the lane narrow, but a hill of dirt was piled on one side. Also in my lights was a man…a big man trying to push his stalled car out of the only lane, over ridges of dirt. All the movements in the scene seemed to be in slow motion. So much was happening, and so fast! Then in my headlights an impossible sight happened. The man lifted the car up with his hands under the bumper and pushed the car out of the lane as all the plunging cars came to a halt, with no room to spare and not a sound of impact. Only I heard my silent, "Thank you, God," as my Angel concluded her latest feat.

As he found the necessary super-human strength in the nick of time, the man in the headlights had at that moment, understandably, lost control of his bladder. I could see the telltale wetness on his trousers. As all the cars slowly moved ahead, I wondered who the man was and if he was all right. There was no side of the road where I could pull over. I'm sure he must have had an angel also, and she took care of everything for him.

Chapter Thirty-Eight

I wrote many pages ago, that I thought remembering my past life was like going to the movies. I could sit and be comfortable, turn down the house lights by closing my eyes; I could not only be the viewer but also the projectionist up in the booth. I put any images on the screen that I want to see, and in any order. We must all be capable of this bit of magic, but for sure the only pictures in the projector would be your own; unless you want to use your imagination. Then you could show any kind of movie you want to see.

As I draw to a close the mental movie of parts of my life that I have been narrating, I realize that I don't really want to turn up the house lights and roll the credits, even though the popcorn is long gone. Seeing all the wonderful shots of my long ago life has been an extreme pleasure, and I hope that it has been pleasurable reading for you. If so, my efforts have been worthwhile, even though I know that you couldn't possibly see it all as well as I could.

Before the theater closes for the night, let me show a few flashback scenes that seem to be tied to the movie just shown. The projector will be rolling on and off through the many years past and the scenes will be in a loose sequence.

⁜ *As a very young boy, I am sitting in the very front row of my neighborhood Presbyterian church, earnestly listening to the minister, Dr. Bowman, preach. I don't remember what he said that Sunday morning, but I remember hearing it and I can see him saying it, and it was a long time ago. The sermon must have been impressive.*

⁜ *We are all in class A uniform, my crew and my best friend, pilot Jack Evarts. Jack is to be my best man, and the wedding is about to begin. What a happy, impossible time it was, and the war seemed so far away! I wish that I could see all the details of the scene more clearly. I can only see the general features.*

⁜ *Gander Field, Newfoundland, was bathed in cold but beautiful sunlight. It was the Sunday morning before we were to take off for our transatlantic flight to the theater of war. I was sitting in church service as if it was on the schedule for*

Vern and me visiting Taj Mahal.

Camel, Vern and me acting like tourists.

Pilot of 5th Liaison Squadron that received the Purple Heart; I wish that I remembered his name....

this very important time of my life. Some of my flying buddies were with me, and I'll bet thoughts in our minds were quite similar as we sang and prayed.

✳ I am sitting on a stone bench talking with a British officer. Along side of me sits my boyhood friend from grammar school. We are in Agra, India, and the stone bench is along side the reflecting pool in front of the Taj Mahal. I had come back to Agra on a weeklong leave to spend some time with my friend, Vern. A fine reunion and a beautifully happy scene.

✳ A sunny Sunday morning is seen. Some friends and I are sitting in a large and once beautiful chapel. I say once beautiful because either bombs or artillery fire blew down the altar end of the church. The Japanese had used the chapel for sheltering their mules and donkeys, and now our forces had covered the open end with hanging parapak chutes. The colored chutes actually looked kinda pretty. The church had been the Roberts Memorial Chapel, Bhamo, Burma, and was in regular use again after our guys took over. We felt a little like being back home in church.

⁜ The whole 5th liaison squadron is assembled on the landing field tarmac in formation and standing at attention while the squadron commander is making a presentation of the Purple Heart to one of our pilots. He was wounded by enemy ground fire while flying low over Japanese troops. Even though wounded, he successfully returned to our base and safely landed his L-5 aircraft.

⁜ Looking out the cockpit window of my C-47, off to the starboard side was a beautiful pagoda type temple, standing out in the sparkling water of a pretty little lake connected with the shore by a narrow causeway.

⁜ Sitting in our bamboo basha with my roommate, learning how to play chess, while listening to a record on the record player. Music playing was "Over the Rainbow" and "Celery Stalks at Midnight" on the other side. Relaxing and having fun.

⁜ Off the side of a runway at a Burma airfield was my airplane #623, that I had flown halfway around the world to the war. It lay there with one wing sticking up in the air. I knew nothing about the circumstances of the crash, but I sure felt sad at the sight of the end of good old #623.

⁜ My crew and I were waiting our turn to take off from Myitkyina Airfield in Burma. We had unloaded our cargo and had been reloaded with cargo for a return flight to our base at Ledo, Assam, India. We watched a converted B-24 bomber attempt a too hot and too high landing, being told by the tower to go around and try again. The B-24 had been converted into a tanker airplane and probably had a full load of aviation fuel. For some reason on its climbing turn to go around for another landing try, the big plane just went one wing down into the ground. Everyone who had an open microphone at the time cried out with groans of disbelief and tearful comment. The huge cloud of flame and smoke wiped out any thought of survivors. Our flight over the scene after takeoff revealed only a monstrous blackened area of ground.

⁜ We are in San Pedro Bay, waiting for the morning fog to lift so that we can dock the great ship and finally get our feet back on the beloved soil of our United States of America. And yes, the fog did lift, and we did tread the sacred ground with hearts full of happiness and thankfulness. After all, we knew how many comrades didn't make the return trip as we did. A sobering thought.

⁜ After a twelve-hour watch on the job as a Pinkerton Security Officer, I was driving home and dead tired. Daytime sleeping was never one of my talents. No matter how darkened my bedroom was, my body could not be fooled into thinking that it should sleep. So after two nights of twelve-hour watches, Saturday and Sunday, I was an accident about to happen. A part-time night job really mixes up days and nights to the point that I couldn't get used to either. At least that was the way it was for me, and I was trying to get home on a Monday morning so I could *jump into bed and get some much-needed sleep. Well, I couldn't wait for the bed and my eyes closed just long enough for me to drive off the road heading for a steep drop-off. Lucky for me, my Angel tapped me on the forehead, woke me up in time to madly swerve back onto the road, thus once again saving my neck and all my other parts.*

✳ After the war at a church service in Green Valley, Arizona, we were having a memorial service for Bill Misek, Ginnie's son and my stepson. He had recently passed away due to a heart attack, at age 52. I was singing the Navy Hymn in his honor. He had served the Navy on the aircraft carrier, the USS Independence. I don't know how I managed to get through that hymn without choking up.

✳ Also, Don Fuller is sitting in the congregation. I didn't know it until after joining the church that he was a member of the famous "Merrill's Marauders." They were fighting the Japanese on the ground while I was flying above them, dropping supplies by parapak. A small world!

It's getting late. The movie is over and the lights are coming up as the credits are rolling. Again I say, "I hope that you enjoyed seeing such a large portion of my life and are somewhat impressed by my Angel. She really was with me throughout my long and wonderful life…and still is.

Thank you with a heartfelt "Hasta La Vista."

Credits From the Author

I thank GOD for my wonderful lifetime containing such a wealth of experiences, acquaintances, and loved ones. This writing touches most of them, and gives credit to my beautiful and lovely Angel for my surprising survival.

Incidentally, my beautiful friend, Angela, has been my editor for this project, and was a very important cog in the machinery. She is also an angel, in my estimation. Speaking of angels, Beth Montgomery was a beautiful model for the artistic creation of "Angel," as shown on our cover, and I am grateful.

Credit must also be given where credit is due:

Michelle, my beautiful illustrator (for great illustrating);

Scott and Anissa, my handsome grandson and beautiful granddaughter (for lots of hard work on copy);

My handsome son Roger, (for patience and love);

My beautiful daughter-in-law Cindy (for love and so much interest);

My beautiful granddaughter Sarah (for so much love);

My handsome grandson Brad (for lots of love);

And my "Burma Buddy," Don Fuller (for not only being handsome, but for being there in the thick of the fighting, as a large part of the success of our mission in Burma. Also, Don's support for my writing efforts was invaluable.)

My Editor, Angela.

My Illustrator, Michelle.

My Burma Buddy, Don,